HOUSES
CASAS
HÄUSER

H KLICZKOWSKI

HOUSES
CASAS
HÄUSER

Idea and Concept/**Idea y concepto**/Idee und Konzept: **Paco Asensio, Hugo Kliczkowski**

Editor and Texts/**Editor y textos**/Verlagskoordination und Text: **Alejandro Bahamón**

Introduction/**Introducción**/Einleitung: **Hugo Kliczkowski**

Art Direction/**Directora de arte**/Art Direktor: **Mireia Casanovas Soley**

Layout/**Maquetación**/Grafik Design: **Ignasi Gracia Blanco, Cris Tarradas**

English translation/**Traducción al inglés**/Übersetzung ins Englische: **Michael Brunelle, Beatriz Cortabarria**

Spanish translation/**Traducción al español**/Übersetzung ins Spanische: **Marta Casado**

German translation/**Traducción al alemán**/Übersetzung ins Deutsche: **Susanne Engler**

Copyright for the international edition/**Copyright para la edición internacional**/Internationales Copyright
© H Kliczkowski-Onlybook, S.L.
La Fundición, 15. Polígono Industrial Santa Ana
28529 Rivas-Vaciamadrid. Madrid. Spain
Tel.: +34 91 666 50 01
Fax: +34 91 301 26 83
onlybook@onlybook.com
www.onlybook.com

Editorial project/**Proyecto editorial**/Verlagsprojekt:

© **LOFT** Publications
Via Laietana 32, 4°Of. 92
08003 Barcelona. Spain
Tel.: +34 932 688 088
Fax: +34 932 687 073
loft@loftpublications.com
www.loftpublications.com

ISBN: 84-96304-43-4 (European edition except UK)
ISBN: 84-96304-57-4 (UK edition)
ISBN: 84-96304-56-6 (USA edition)

DL: B. 38.182-2004

Printed by/**Impreso en**/Gedruckt in:
Egedsa. Barcelona, Spain

> Summary

> Índice

> Inhalt

© Anriet Denis

"I eagerly search for houses that are 'houses for people' and not houses for architects. It is an important quest. One can say that a house for people emanates love. Allow me to explain this from a filmmaker's point of view; imagine being in a restaurant, not one of those fancy restaurants where the arbitrary intervention of the waiters and the sommeliers destroy my poem, but one of those quaint, small cafés where two or three patrons have just finished drinking their coffees and are chatting.

The plates, glasses, bottles, the salt, the pepper, the napkins, napkin holder... are all still on the table. Observe the total disarray in the relationships between these objects; they have served their purpose, they have all been handled by one guest or another. The distances that separate them represent the measure of daily life. It is a mathematically coherent composition; there is no wrong place in the choice of placement, no hiatus, no false intentions. If a film director who was not contaminated by Hollywood were there at that moment, filming a close up of that still life it would be a testament to pure harmony. Could this be possible? Yes, and how unfortunate are those who seek the false, pretentious, commercial, and academic harmony of Vignola circa 1925, or of the latest fad.

"Busco con verdadero afán esas casas que son 'casas de hombres' y no casas de arquitectos. El asunto es grave. Puede decirse que una casa de hombres es amor. Dejadme precisar por esto lo que respecta al cine, observad un día, no en uno de esos restaurantes de lujo, en los cuales la intervención arbitraria de los camareros y de los "sommeliers" destruye mi poema, observad en una pequeña taberna popular, dos o tres comensales que han acabado de tomar su café y están charlando.

La mesa todavía esta llena de vasos, botellas, platos, la aceitera, la sal, la pimienta, la servilleta y el servilletero, etc. Ved el orden fatal que pone todos estos objeto en relación los unos con los otros; todos han servido; han sido cogidos con la mano de uno o de otro de los comensales, las distancias que los separan son la medida de la vida. Es una composición matemáticamente arreglada; no hay ningún falso lugar, ni un hiatus, ni un engaño. Si un cineasta no alucinado por Hollywood se encontrase ahí, filmando esta naturaleza muerta en 'primer plano' tendríamos un testimonio de pura armonía ¿Es posible? Sí, y desgraciados aquellos que buscan falsas armonías, trucadas, comerciales, armonías académicas de Vignola, de 1925 o de última moda".

„Ich suche mit großem Eifer nach den Häusern, die "Häuser von Menschen", und nicht Häuser von Architekten sind. Das ist eine wirklich ernste Angelegenheit. Man kann sagen, dass ein Haus von Menschen Liebe ist. Lasst mich deshalb ein Beispiel aus dem Kino anführen. Beobachten Sie einen Tagen, aber nicht in einem dieser Luxusrestaurants, in denen das eigenmächtige Eingreifen der Kellner und der „Sommeliers" mein Gedicht zerstört, sondern eine kleine, beliebte Kneipe, in der zwei oder drei Tischgäste gerade ihren Kaffee beendet haben und sich noch ein wenig unterhalten.

Der Tisch ist noch voller Gläser, Flaschen, Teller, die Ölflasche, das Salz, der Pfeffer, die Servietten, der Serviettenhalter, usw. Betrachten Sie die unausweichliche Ordnung, die alle diese Objekte untereinander haben; alle haben zu etwas gedient, alle wurden von der Hand des einen oder anderen Tischgastes aufgenommen, die Abstände, die zwischen ihnen existieren, sind aus dem Leben gegriffene Maße. Es handelt sich um eine mathematisch angeordnete Komposition, es gibt keinen falschen Platz, keinen Hiatus, keine Täuschung. Falls sich ein Cineast, der nicht von Hollywood geblendet ist, hier befände und dieses Stillleben „im Vordergrund" filmen würde, hätten wir ein Zeugnis der reinen Harmonie. Ist das möglich? Ja, und unglücklich sind die, die nach den falschen Harmonien suchen, den vorgetäuschten, kommerziellen, akademischen Harmonien von Vignola im Jahr 1925 oder der letzten Mode".

Le Corbusier, in his 1929 American prologue for Precisions

Le Corbusier, en el prólogo americano de la edición de 1929 de Precisiones

Le Corbusier, im Amerikanischen Prolog 1929, Precisiones

Unité d'Habitation © Anriet Denis

Books, Houses, Cities, and Architects

Why this book?

Because we like to look at houses and design plans, and we love to edit them. A desire (not always possible) is to attract the interest of the reader. We must confess that after so many years in the publishing profession, we truly do not know how to achieve that. We have some ideas and some convictions as well, and we rely on them. We do not know and we do not expect to find out when and why a person chooses a book and, by chance, decides to take it home. We could imagine that it is to share some dream. And that dream, in this case, is a house, a plan, a living space.

And we ask ourselves:

Is an empty house inviting enough to justify this? Does a space that is not our own stimulate our desire to learn more about it? Can a house, wherever it may be, serve as an inspiration and as a model for a similar one?

Is its cost, even if it does not fit our budget, an obstacle for desiring it, or do we want it precisely because it is unattainable?

Desires, fantasies, ambitions, status symbol or not, houses are central to our dreams, and fundamentally, a basic necessity.

Libros, casas, ciudades y arquitectos

¿Por qué este libro?

Porque nos gusta ver casas y proyectos y nos apasiona editarlos. Un deseo (no siempre posible) es conseguir atraer el interés de los lectores. Podemos confesar que después de tantos años en el mundo editorial, sinceramente, no sabemos cómo se consigue esto. Tenemos algunas ideas, algunas certezas también y por ellas apostamos. No sabemos ni podemos saber cuándo y por qué un lector escoge un libro y se lo lleva –casualmente– a su casa. Podemos pensar que es para compartir algún sueño. Y ese sueño, en este caso, será una casa, un proyecto, un espacio habitable.

Y nos interrogamos:

Una casa que no habitamos, ¿nos invita a hacerlo? Un entorno que no es el nuestro, ¿nos estimula a conocerlo? Una casa, dondequiera que esté, ¿nos interesa como modelo para otras similares? Si el coste no se ajusta a nuestras posibilidades, ¿es un obstáculo para desearla, o por el contrario, la queremos justamente por ser inalcanzable?

Deseos, fantasías, ambiciones, ilusiones, símbolo de posición social o no, las casas son una parte central de nuestros sueños y, básicamente, una necesidad vital.

Bücher, Häuser, Städte und Architekten

Warum dieses Buch?

Da wir uns gerne Häuser und Pläne anschauen, und sie leidenschaftlich gerne veröffentlichen. Unser Wunsch ist es (was nicht immer möglich ist), auch das Interesse der Leser damit zu wecken. Wir müssen aber zugeben, dass wir nach so vielen Jahren in der Verlagswelt eigentlich immer noch nicht wissen, wie man das macht. Wir haben da ein paar Ideen und auch einige Gewissheiten, und auf diese setzen wir. Wir wissen nicht und können nicht wissen, wann und warum ein Leser ein Buch auswählt und es, ganz zufällig, nach Hause mitnimmt. Wir könnten denken, dass vielleicht Träume darin verwickelt sind. Und diese Träume sind in diesem Fall ein Haus, eine Projekt, ein Raum zum Wohnen.

Und wir stellen uns ein paar Fragen:

Ein Haus, in dem wir nicht wohnen, lädt es uns zum darin Wohnen ein? Eine Umgebung, die nicht unsere ist, würden wir sie gerne kennen lernen? Ein Haus, egal, wo es sich befindet, ist es für uns ein interessantes Modell für andere, ähnliche Häuser? Wenn die Kosten nicht unseren Möglichkeiten entsprechen, ist es ein Hindernis, um es uns zu wünschen, oder wollen wir es im Gegenteil, weil es unerreichbar ist?

Wünsche, Phantasien, Ambitionen, Illusionen, Symbol für die gesellschaftliche Stellung oder nicht, Häuser bilden einen Teil unserer Träume, und vor allen Dingen sind sie lebensnotwendig.

Villa Rotonda © Pino Guidolotti

Villa Rotonda © Pino Guidolotti

Houses, Cities, and Architects

House, can, casa, maison, logis, home, haus, shack, vohnung, building, apartment, loft, penthouse, duplex, residence, etcetera.

Yet another question: is a house a building to live in? "A house is a home", Le Corbusier used to proclaim. He also proposed the idea that a house can be a machine to live in.

A house can be so many other things as well, since it constitutes the unit that, together with other elements, shapes and gives meaning to the urban environment, to the city.

And it is the latter that shapes the character of a house, therefore we ask, do the two interact?

Andrea Palladio (1508-1580) wrote in chapter twelve of his Book II that "a city is nothing more than a large house, and on the other hand, a house is nothing more than a small city."

We live in and inhabit houses, we dream about them, we imagine them, and we think about them as described by the great master Frank Lloyd Wright (1869-1959).

"Thinking is dealing with simplicity, and that means thinking of the whole as a single vision..." And he added in referring to the project, that drawing "five lines where three are sufficient is simply foolish."

But what do those houses look like? Are they like the others? And which others? Different, personal, we know that often they are more than a reflection of our needs. Luckily.

Casas, ciudades y arquitectos

Casa, can, house, maison, logis, home, haus, choza, wohnung, edificio, piso, loft, penthouse, dúplex, vivienda, etcétera.

Más preguntas: ¿es la casa un edificio para habitar? "Una casa es un hogar", nos hacía pensar Le Corbusier, y planteaba que una casa puede ser también una máquina de habitar.

Es, además, otras cosas, ya que la casa se constituye en la unidad que conforma y da sentido, junto a otros programas, a la urbe, a la ciudad.

Y es esta última la que da carácter a la casa. ¿Interactúan ambas?

Andrea Palladio (1508-1580) escribía en en el capítulo 12 de su Libro II "la ciudad no es otra cosa que una casa grande y, por el contrario, la casa es una ciudad pequeña".

Vivimos y habitamos en casas, soñamos, nos imaginamos y pensamos en ellas en el sentido que le asignaba el maestro Frank Lloyd Wright (1869-1959). "Pensar es pactar con la sencillez, y eso significa pensar con una visión única para el conjunto..." Y agregaba refiriéndose al proyecto que trazar "cinco líneas donde tres son suficientes es simplemente una estupidez".

¿Pero cómo son esas casas? ¿Son como las otras? ¿Y qué otras? Distintas, personales, sabemos que muchas veces son algo más que el reflejo de nuestras necesidades. Por suerte.

Häuser, Städte und Architekten

Casa, can, house, maison, logis, home, Haus, choza, Wohnung, edificio, piso, loft, penthouse, duplex, vivienda, usw...

Noch mehr Fragen: Ist ein Haus ein Gebäude zum Wohnen?

„Ein Haus ist ein Heim", ließ uns Le Corbusier denken, und er warf gleichzeitig das Problem auf, dass ein Haus auch eine Wohnmaschine sein kann.

Es kann auch noch etwas anderes sein, da das Haus in einer Einheit entsteht, die zusammen mit anderen Elementen, die Stadt bildet, und ihr Sinn gibt.

Und es ist die Stadt, die dem Haus seinen Charakter verleiht. Gibt es eine Wechselbeziehung zwischen beiden?

Andrea Palladio (1508-1580) schrieb im 12. Kapitel seines 2. Buches „Die Stadt ist nichts anderes als ein großes Haus und, im Gegensatz dazu, das Haus ist eine kleine Stadt".

Wir leben und wohnen in Häusern, wir träumen, wir stellen sie uns vor und wir denken an sie in dem Sinne, den der Meister Frank Lloyd Wright (1869-1959) aufzeigte.

„Denken bedeutet, einen Pakt mit der Einfachheit abschließen, und das bedeutet mit einer einzigen Vision für das Gesamte zu denken..." Und er fügte hinzu, wobei er sich auf die Planung bezog, dass beim Zeichnen, „fünf Linien dort, wo drei ausreichen würden, dies einfach dumm ist".

There are people who wish to live in cities like Priene, conforming to the concepts of geometric regularity of Hipodamo de Mileto, in the transitional era between Classicism and Hellenism?

Or would they like living in houses like those in the Fachada Delta project (1954) or Barrio de Xul Solar (1953), (Óscar Agustín Alejandro Schulz Solari, 1887-1963).

Or prefer the houses in Paris where Juan Gris (José Victoriano González, 1887-1927) used to teach.

Or in the DOM-INO House (1916) by Le Corbusier (Charles Édouard Jeanneret-Gris, 1887-1965), or in his apartment buildings in Marseilles, Nantes-Rezé; Briey-en-Fôret; Berlin-Charlottenburg and Firminy-Vert, applying the laws of harmony of his modular.

Or living in Villa Mairea (1937) by Finnish architect Alvar Aalto (1898-1976).

A book, this book about houses, our houses, the houses that others live in, bordering what could be considered their own parameters, show examples, and perhaps prototypes.

We say prototypes because when we speak of houses we also refer to behaviors, to styles, and ultimately, to culture.

This is especially true if we look at them as lifestyles and customs, the knowledge of an era, a social group. A reader looks at the book and sees the houses: does he or she look at them and see them with the purpose of choosing one, or to learn, by inference, what other people have desired?

Habrá quien desee vivir en ciudades como Priene, siguiendo los conceptos de regularidad geométrica de Hipodamo de Mileto, en aquellas épocas de transición entre la edad clásica y el helenismo.

O en casas como las del proyecto Fachada Delta (1954) o Barrio (1953) de Xul Solar (Óscar Agustín Alejandro Schulz Solari, 1887-1963).

O en las casas de París que enseñaba Juan Gris (José Victoriano González, 1887-1927).

O en la casa DOM-INO (1916) de Le Corbusier (Charles Édouard Jeanneret-Gris, 1887-1965), o en sus unidades habitacionales de Marsella, Nantes-Rezé; Briey-en-Fôret; Berlin-Charlottenburg y Firminy-Vert, dejándose llevar por las leyes armoniosas del modulor.

O vivir en la Villa Mairea (1937) del arquitecto finlandés Alvar Aalto (1898-1976).

Un libro, este libro sobre casas, nuestras casas, las casas que habitan otros, bordeando lo que pueden ser los propios parámetros, exhibe ejemplos, quizás prototipos.

Prototipos, porque cuando hablamos de casas también hablamos de comportamientos, de estilos, en definitiva, de cultura.

Sobre todo si la entendemos como el conjunto de modos de vida y costumbres, de los conocimientos de una época, de un grupo social.

Un lector mira el libro, ve las casas, ¿las mira y las ve con actitud de escoger?, ¿o para saber, deduciendo, qué han deseado otras personas?

Aber wie sind diese Häuser? Sind sie wie die anderen? Und welche anderen? Anders, persönlich, wir wissen, dass sie oft mehr als die Widerspiegelung unserer Bedürfnisse sind. Zum Glück.

Es gibt Menschen, die in Städten wie Priene leben möchten, und die den Konzepten der geometrischen Regelmäßigkeit von Hippodamos von Milet folgen, in jenen Epochen des Übergangs von der Klassik zum Hellenismus.

Oder in Häusern wie die des Projektes Fachada Delta (1954) oder Barrio (1953) von Xul Solar (Óscar Agustín Alejandro Schulz Solari, 1887-1963).

Oder in den Häusern von Paris, die Juan Gris (José Victoriano González, 1887-1927) zeigte.

Oder in dem Haus DOM-INO (1916) von Le Corbusier (Charles Édouard Jeanneret-Gris, 1887-1965), oder in seinen Wohneinheiten in Marseille, Nantes-Rezé; Briey-en-Fôret; Berlin-Charlottenburg und Firminy-Vert, um sich von den harmonischen Gesetzen des Modularen hinreißen zu lassen.

Oder in der Villa Mairea (1937) des finnischen Architekten Alvar Aalto (1898-1976).

Ein Buch, unser Buch über Häuser, unsere Häuser, die Häuser, in denen andere wohnen, das sich dem annähert, was die Parameter selbst sein könnten, zeigt Beispiele, vielleicht Prototypen.

Prototypen, da wir, wenn wir über Häuser reden, auch über Verhaltensweisen, Stile, und letzten Endes über Kultur reden.

As far back as 1919 Walter Gropius (1883-1969) had a vision, to which he assigned a technical name, Bauhaus (house under construction), because he believed that a house was "synonymous with a wealth of ideas, precision in its execution, and capability of adaptation."

A house is an interpretation of life and the surrounding environment, a human and created environment.

Gropius agreed with his peers that a house promotes reflection and the development of future society, when understood in more of an individual context than a social one.

We are what we build, what we live in.

When we look at the projects in this book we smile thinking about classical Greece where artists were famous and well respected, where their personal talents, not their social origins, gave them prestige. Unlike those times, the architects and artists of later Hellenistic periods admitted that their function was more contemplative than practical. The purpose of their art and architecture was to represent reality, not to modify it.

And during the Roman period, the status of artists was even lower, the designer was mistaken for a contractor or an worker, a situation that lasted until the Middle Ages.

Ya en 1919, Walter Gropius (1883-1969) tuvo una visión a la que puso un nombre programático, Bauhaus (casa en construcción), porque pensaba que casa era "sinónimo de riqueza de ideas, exactitud de ejecución y capacidad de adaptación".

La casa como interpretación de la vida y del entorno. Entorno humano y construido.

Gropius acordaba con sus pares que la casa constituía un impulso para la reflexión y el desarrollo futuro de la sociedad, entendida en forma más social que individual.

Somos en tanto que construimos, en tanto que habitamos.

Al ver estos proyectos, nos sonreímos al pensar que en la época clásica, los artistas eran personajes famosos y respetados y que eran sus dotes personales y no su origen social lo que les daba o no prestigio.

A diferencia de los griegos, los arquitectos y artistas del período helenístico reconocen que su función es más contemplativa que práctica, la arquitectura y el arte en el período helenístico sirve para representar la realidad, no para modificarla.

Es en la época romana, donde la consideración social de los artistas es aún más baja, el diseñador se confunde con los constructores o ejecutores y esta situación continúa en la Edad Media.

Hans Hollein (1934) wies darauf hin, dass für ihn „die Architektur nicht nur einfach die Lösung eines gegebenen Problems ist, sondern so eine Art Meinung". Häuser sind, wie wir bereits wissen, etwas mehr als Bauten, sie sind Ikonen, und so zeigen wir sie. Oft zeigen wir uns MIT ihnen, und andere Male zeigen wir uns IN ihnen.

Schon 1919 hatte Walter Gropius (1883-1969) eine Vision, der er einen programmatischen Namen gab, Bauhaus, da er der Ansicht war, dass Haus „gleichbedeutend mit Ideenreichtum, Genauigkeit der Ausführung und Anpassungsfähigkeit" sei.

Das Haus als Interpretation des Lebens und der Umwelt. Menschliche und bebaute Umwelt.

Gropius vereinbarte mit den Seinen, dass ein Haus einen Impuls zum Nachdenken und zur Entwicklung der Zukunft der Gesellschaft sei, da man eher sozial als individuell verstehen sollte.

Wir sind genauso das, was wir bauen, wie das, was wir bewohnen.

Wenn man also die Häuser in diesem Band sieht, lächeln wir bei dem Gedanken, dass im klassischen Griechenland die Künstler berühmte und respektierte Persönlichkeiten waren, und dass es ihr persönliches Talent und nicht ihre gesellschaftliche Herkunft war, das sie berühmt machte.

Im Gegensatz zu jener Zeit erkannten die Architekten und Künstler der späteren, hellenistischen Epoche an, dass ihre Funktion eher kontemplativ als praktisch sei, ihre Architektur und ihre Kunst dienten zur

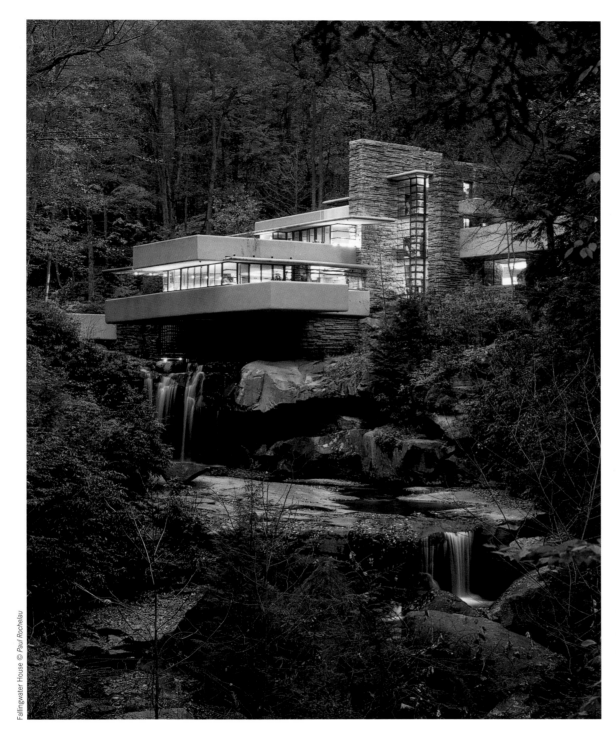

Fallingwater House © Paul Rochelau

Since this confusion still prevails, the same description would still be valid today.
And thinking about the future, how will it be, what will our books be like, our houses, our cities?

"...nothing that comes from the past can be reborn, but it will never disappear completely either..."

Painters and Masons, Jousimies, 1921

Como esta confusión continúa, uno podría hacer la misma descripción hoy en día.
Y pensar ¿cómo será mañana?, ¿como serán nuestros libros?, ¿nuestras casas?, ¿nuestras ciudades?

"... nada de lo que viene del pasado puede renacer, pero tampoco desaparecerá por completo..."

Painters and Masons, Jousimies, 1921

Darstellung der Wirklichkeit, und nicht dazu, sie zu verändern.
Und in der Zeit der Römer war die gesellschaftliche Anerkennung der Künstler sogar noch geringer. Der Planer wird mit dem Erbauer oder dem Ausführenden verwechselt, diese Situation ändert sich bis zum Mittelalter nicht.

Da diese Verwechslung auch noch weiterhin besteht, könnte man heutzutage die gleiche Beschreibung geben.
Und denken: Wie wird es morgen sein? Wir werden unsere Bücher sein? Unsere Häuser? Unsere Städte?

„....nichts, was aus der Vergangenheit kommt, kann wieder geboren werden, aber es verschwindet auch nicht vollständig..."

Painters and Masons, Jousimies, 1921

Hugo Alberto Kliczkowski Juritz

HOUSES

CASAS / HÄUSER

☐ This house is located in the Alto de Pinheiros area of the Brazilian city of São Paulo. According to the architect, São Paulo is possibly the least attractive city in the world, a large urban complex where chaos and disorder reign, and where the architecture is almost always unrelated to its setting. This project is no exception; it takes the form of a large white perimeter wall that wraps around the property, isolating it from its context and creating its own views facing the house. The clients are a couple working in the field of advertising, and early in the process they specified the things that should drive the design project. These included a very large shelf that would occupy the double-height living room, large-scale windows that open to the garden, a long swimming pool, a kitchen complete with an orange dining table in the center, two symmetrical marble stairways framed by natural light, a custom-designed studio; and sophisticated spaces with elegant proportions that are permanently linked with the exterior.

Gama-Issa House

› Marcio Kogan

São Paulo, Brazil › 2001 › Photos © Arnaldo Pappalardo

☐ Esta casa se localiza en la zona de Alto de Pinherios, en la ciudad brasileña de São Paulo que, según el propio arquitecto, es quizás la ciudad menos bella del mundo. Un gran complejo urbano en el que reina el caos y el desorden, por lo que pocas veces un proyecto arquitectónico establece algún diálogo con su entorno. El caso de este proyecto no es una excepción, se trata de un gran envoltorio blanco en forma de muro perimetral que aísla

☐ Dieses Haus befindet sich im Viertel Alto de Pinheiros in der brasilianischen Stadt São Paulo, die, wie der Architekt sagt, vielleicht die hässlichste Stadt der Welt ist. Eine riesige Stadt, in der Chaos und Unordnung herrschen und in der nur sehr selten die architektonische Planung im Dialog mit der Umgebung steht. Der Fall dieses Gebäudes ist somit keine Ausnahme. Es handelt sich um eine große, weiße Hülle in Form einer Mauer, die das

la propiedad del contexto en el que se ubica para crear un propio paisaje hacia el que se vuelca la casa. Los clientes, una pareja que trabaja en el sector de la publicidad, planteó desde un principio el programa que debía solucionar el proyecto: una estantería de grandes dimensiones que ocupara toda la sala de estar con techos a doble altura, ventanales de gran formato que se abren al jardín, una piscina longitudinal, una cocina que albergara una mesa de comedor naranja en el centro, dos escaleras simétricas de mármol demarcadas por la luz natural, un estudio diseñado a medida y, en general, espacios sofisticados, de proporciones elegantes que se relacionan permanentemente con el exterior.

Haus von seiner Umwelt isoliert. Innerhalb dieser Mauern wird eine eigene Landschaft geschaffen, die sich bis zum Haus erstreckt. Die Kunden, ein Paar, das im Werbesektor tätig ist, hatten schon von Anfang an sehr genaue Vorstellungen von dem, was sie sich für ihr Haus wünschten: Ein riesiges Regal, das sich über das gesamte Wohnzimmer mit einer Decke in doppelter Höhe erstreckt, große Fenster, die sich zum Garten hin öffnen, einen längs verlaufenden Swimmingpool, eine Küche, in deren Mitte ein orangener Esstisch stehen sollte, zwei symmetrisch verlaufende Marmortreppen, auf die Tageslicht fällt, ein auf Maß gearbeitetes Atelier und im allgemeinen edle Räume in eleganten Proportionen, die ständig mit außen in Verbindung stehen sollten.

› **Ground floor**

› Planta baja

› Erdegeschoss

› **First floor**

› Planta primera

› Erster Stock

0   2   4

Marcio Kogan graduated from the Mackenzie School of Architecture in 1976. Since that time he has received many awards for different architectural assignments. He has designed a variety of small-scale and large-scale projects, mainly in São Paulo, Brazil and the surrounding area. His architectural work is known for its strong, refined lines. Since 1974 he combines architecture projects with his passion for the cinema. He has created a great number of short films, and his first full-length movie was made in 1988.

Marcio Kogan se graduó en la Escuela de Arquitectura Mackenzie en 1976 y desde entonces ha recibido numerosos premios por varias de sus obras arquitectónicas. Ha diseñado una amplia variedad de proyectos de pequeña y gran escala, principalmente en São Paulo, Brasil, y sus alrededores. Su trabajo como arquitecto, en donde destaca una depurada y contundente línea de diseño, lo combina desde 1974 con su pasión por el cine, disciplina en la que ha realizado numerosos cortometrajes y un primer largo en 1988.

Marcio Kogan schloss sein Studium 1976 an der Mackenzie School of Architecture ab und ist seitdem mit zahlreichen Preisen für seine Arbeiten ausgezeichnet worden. Er hat eine ganze Reihe kleiner und großer Gebäude hauptsächlich in São Paulo, Brasilien, und Umgebung entworfen. Seine Arbeit als Architekt ist vor allem von der Klarheit und Überzeugungskraft seiner Entwürfe gekennzeichnet, die er seit 1974 mit seiner Leidenschaft für das Kino kombiniert. Er hat für eine ganze Reihe von Kurzfilmen und auch bereits 1988 für einen Spielfilm Regie geführt.

According to the architects, this house is the result of an in-depth exploration of the different ways of relating to the views — those of the house as well as those that can be seen from it. The project is located on an elevated site with a view of the city of Melbourne on one side and a view of the nearby suburbs on the other. The relevance of these two views is embodied in the house in the form of a break in the large copper façade, which also creates the dramatic feeling of the high interior ceiling. The subtle details of the layout create different kinds of relationships between the various rooms and between the interior and exterior as well. The two-level structure is supported by a large concrete shell, which acts as a base and as a transition to the ground. The pool, the garage, a wine cellar, a storage room, and the access ramp are all located inside this base. The main part of the building, which looks much lighter, is made of a wood and metal frame and very light covering materials that filter the natural light.

City Hill House

› John Wardle Architects

Melbourne, Australia › 2003 › Photos © Trevor Mein

☐ Esta casa se convirtió para los arquitectos en toda una exploración sobre las diferentes maneras de relacionar las vistas, tanto de la propia vivienda como las que se extienden fuera de ella. El proyecto se emplaza en un solar elevado que presenta, por un lado, panorámicas de la ciudad de Melbourne y, por el otro, vistas de los suburbios más cercanos. Los ejes de estas dos circunstancias se manifiestan en la volumetría de la construcción en

☐ Mit diesem Gebäude erforschten die Architekten verschiedene Methoden, um den Ausblick zu integrieren, sowohl innerhalb als auch außerhalb des Hauses. Das Gebäude befindet sich auf einem erhöhten Grundstück mit einem ausgezeichneten Blick über die Stadt Melbourne auf der einen Seite und auf die Vororte der Stadt auf der anderen. Die Achsen dieser beiden Faktoren wurden in der Volumetrie des Gebäudes so

forma de una abertura ejecutada en la gran fachada revestida de cobre, que al mismo tiempo determina el carácter dramático de la doble altura interior. Los sutiles giros que presenta la composición general crean diferentes tipos de relaciones entre las diferentes estancias así como entre el interior y el exterior. La estructura de dos plantas está apoyada sobre una vasta envoltura de hormigón que sirve de base y volumen transitorio con el terreno. En esta base se ubican la piscina, el garaje, una bodega, el almacén y la rampa de acceso. El volumen principal, de aspecto mucho más ligero, está formado por una estructura de metal y madera que sirve de marco a revestimientos muy ligeros que filtran la luz natural.

umgesetzt, dass ein Bruch in der großen, mit Kupfer verkleideten Fassade entsteht, die gleichzeitig der doppelten Höhe im Inneren ihren dramatischen Charakter verleiht. Die leichten Drehungen im Gesamtbild schaffen verschiedene Beziehungen zwischen den einzelnen Räumen und zwischen innen und außen. Die zweistöckige Struktur stützt sich auf eine große Betonschale, die gleichzeitig die Basis und der Durchgang auf dem Grundstück ist. Darin befinden sich der Swimmingpool, die Garage, ein Weinkeller, ein Lagerraum und eine Zugangsrampe. Der Hauptteil des Gebäudes wirkt viel leichter und besteht aus einer Holz- und Metallstruktur, die als Rahmen für sehr leichte Verkleidungen dient, durch die sich das Tageslicht filtert.

0   10   20

› Ground floor

› Planta baja

› Erdegeschoss

› First floor

› Planta primera

› Erster Stock

› Sketch

› Croquis

› Skizze

1. What historical reference in particular inspires you when designing a residence?
¿Qué referente histórico en particular le sirve de fuente de inspiración a la hora de proyectar una vivienda?
Welche historische Referenz dient Ihnen als Inspiration beim Entwurf eines Hauses?

2. What is the main factor taken into consideration when designing a residence?
¿Cuál es el principal factor determinante a la hora de diseñar una vivienda?
Welche Rahmenbedingungen, bzw. Faktoren sind für Sie ausschlaggebend beim Konzipieren?

3. What room inside the home do you find most interesting to design?
¿Qué estancia de la vivienda encuentra usted más interesante para diseñar?
Welchen Raum des Hauses finden Sie am spannendsten zu entwerfen?

4. What is your criteria for choosing materials and finishings in a particular room?
¿Cuál es su criterio a la hora de seleccionar los materiales y los acabados en esta estancia?
Welche Kriterien wenden Sie bei der Entscheidung über Materialen und Oberflächen in diesem Raum an?

---

1. The personal histories of our clients are intertwined with the history of the site, its physical characteristics, the region and its social history.

2. Each client and each site requires a unique response. The stage-management of views is always an important consideration.

3. Common to many of our projects is a notion of interrupting continuous space with devices and objects rather than compartmentalizing with walls.

4. The sensual aspect of materials and finishes, recognising the sense of touch in the process of design and manufacture. We aspire to create buildings that reflect the perception of our physical world in its vast and diverse phenomena, in the aesthetic experience of surface.

---

1. Las historias personales de nuestros clientes se entrelazan con la historia del lugar, sus características físicas, la región y su historia social.

2. Cada cliente y cada lugar requiere una única respuesta. El manejo de las visuales, por ejemplo, es una consideración importante.

3. Un rasgo común de nuestros proyectos es la noción de un espacio continuo e interrumpido por mecanismos y objetos, más que creando compartimentos con paredes.

4. El aspecto sensual de los materiales y los acabados y reconocer el sentido del tacto en el proceso de diseño y fabricación. Nosotros aspiramos a crear edificios que reflejen la percepción de nuestro mundo físico y su vasta diversidad de superficies.

---

1. Die persönliche Geschichte unserer Kunden verflechtet sich mit der Geschichte des Ortes, seinen physischen Eigenschaften, der Region und ihrer sozialen Geschichte.

2. Jeder Kunde und jeder Ort braucht eine einzige Antwort. Zum Beispiel der Umgang mit der Sicht, sowohl drinnen als auch draußen, ist ein wichtiger Gesichtspunkt.

3. Ein gemeinsamer Zug unserer Projekte ist die Vorstellung eines durchgehenden Raums, der eher von Mechanismen und Objekten unterbrochen, als dass er durch Wände eingeteilt wird.

4. Das sinnliche Aussehen der Materialien und Oberflächen, wobei der Tastsinn im Gestaltungs und Herstellungsprozess eine Rolle spielt. Wir versuchen, Gebäude zu schaffen, die unsere Wahrnehmung der physischen Welt und die große Vielfalt an Oberflächen widerspiegeln.

John Wardle Architects was founded in 1986, and at the present time it includes 21 professionals from diverse disciplines who collaborate on developing ideas for each project. The firm's uniqueness stems from the variety of projects that it has undertaken all over Australia. Their design portfolio includes single-family homes, apartment towers, university buildings, offices, and shopping malls. The architects work at incorporating the collective and individual characteristics of their clients to enrich and personalize every project.

La firma John Wardle Architects, fundada en 1986 por el propio Wardle, se compone en la actualidad de 21 profesionales que colaboran en diversas disciplinas para desarrollar las ideas que reciben de cada encargo. La particularidad de la compañía radica en la amplia variedad de escalas de proyectos que llevan a cabo por toda Australia. Su obra abarca casas unifamiliares, torres de apartamentos, edificios para universidades, oficinas y centros comerciales. Las características colectivas y particulares de cada cliente se aprovechan para enriquecer y personalizar cada proyecto.

Das Unternehmen John Wardle Architects wurde 1986 von Wardle selbst gegründet. Heute arbeiten 21 Fachleute verschiedener Disziplinen in diesem Büro, die gemeinsam Projekte entwickeln. Was dieses Unternehmen so besonders macht, ist die Tatsache, dass es in ganz Australien bereits sehr verschiedenartige Planungen durchgeführt hat. Dazu gehören Einfamilienhäuser, Mehrfamilienhäuser, Universitätsgebäude, Bürohäuser und Einkaufszentren. Die kollektiven und individuellen Eigenschaften jedes Kunden werden dazu benutzt, die einzelnen Projekte persönlicher zu gestalten und zu bereichern.

☐ This house is located in Honda, Colombia. This dwelling is a combination of two properties facing the street that used to house residential and storage buildings. Only the façades and a few colonial period stonewalls were preserved and incorporated into the project. The climate is very hot year round because the city is at sea level and in the tropical zone. This second home for three associates was conceived as a sequence of open, covered spaces located inside the existing structure. The floor plan is based on sight lines, which convey a labyrinth-like feeling. Every room faces one of the exterior areas, each representing a particular theme: a patio with aromatic herbs, a garden of citrus trees, a rock garden, and a patio with red peppers. Water acts as a unifying element, in the form of a pool, a fountain, or a pond. The lighting, designed by Guillermo Arias, is a key element of the project, enhancing the character of the original walls, the textures, the vegetation, and the water elements.

House in Honda

› Guillermo Arias + Luis Cuartas

Honda, Colombia › 2003 › Photos © Eduardo Consuegra

☐ Esta vivienda, situada en Honda, Colombia, está formada por la unión de dos parcelas que contenían antiguamente viviendas y almacenes que daban a la calle. Sólo se conservaban las fachadas y algunos muros coloniales de piedra que se incorporaron en el proyecto. Por estar casi a nivel del mar y en una zona tropical, el clima presenta temperaturas muy elevadas durante todo el año. Esta segunda residencia para tres socios fue concebida

☐ Dieses Gebäude befindet sich in Honda, in Kolumbien. Dieses Haus entstand durch die Vereinigung zweier Parzellen, auf denen sich einst Wohn- und Lagerhäuser zur Straße hin befanden. Nur die koloniale Fassade und die Steinmauern sind erhalten und wurden in die Planung miteinbezogen. Da sich das Gebäude beinahe auf Höhe des Meeresspiegel und in einer Region mit tropischem Klima befindet, ist die Temperatur das ganze Jahr über

como una secuencia de espacios abiertos y cubiertos, desarrollados a partir de la estructura encontrada, generando una sensación laberíntica pero ordenada a través de ejes visuales. Los espacios están enfocados siempre hacia algún espacio exterior con un carácter específico: un patio de hierbas aromáticas, un jardín de cítricos y otro de piedras o un patio de ajíes. El agua sirve como elemento unificador, en forma de piscina, fuentes o estanques. La iluminación, a cargo de Guillermo Arias, es un elemento determinante en el proyecto para subrayar el carácter de los muros originales, las texturas, la vegetación o los elementos de agua.

sehr hoch. Dieses Ferienhaus für drei Partner wurde als eine Sequenz von offenen und geschlossenen Räumen entworfen, die auf der bereits vorhandenen Struktur beruhen. So hat man das Gefühl, sich in einem Labyrinth zu befinden, das über visuelle Achsen geordnet ist. Alle Räume sind auf einen Gartenbereich mit spezifischem Charakter hin ausgerichtet: ein Innenhof mit Duft- und Würzkräutern, ein Garten mit Orangen- und Zitronenbäumen, ein Steingarten und ein Hof voller Pfeffersträucher. Das Wasser dient als vereinigendes Element, in Form eines Swimmingpools, eines Brunnens und eines Teiches. Die Beleuchtung, die von Guillermo Arias entworfen wurde, ist ein entscheidendes Gestaltungselement, das den Charakter der alten Mauern, die Textur, die Vegetation und die Wasser-Elemente unterstreicht.

0   5   10

› **Ground floor**

› Planta baja

› Erdegeschoss

› **First floor**

› Planta primera

› Erster Stock

› **Roof plan**

› Planta de cubiertas

› Dachgrundriss

0   3   6

› Sections

› Secciones

› Schnitte

› Axonometry

› Axonometría

› Axonometrie

1. What historical reference in particular inspires you when designing a residence?
¿Qué referente histórico en particular le sirve de fuente de inspiración a la hora de proyectar una vivienda?
Welche historische Referenz dient Ihnen als Inspiration beim Entwurf eines Hauses?

2. What is the main factor taken into consideration when designing a residence?
¿Cuál es el principal factor determinante a la hora de diseñar una vivienda?
Welche Rahmenbedingungen, bzw. Faktoren sind für Sie ausschlaggebend beim Konzipieren?

3. What room inside the home do you find most interesting to design?
¿Qué estancia de la vivienda encuentra usted más interesante para diseñar?
Welchen Raum des Hauses finden Sie am spannendsten zu entwerfen?

4. What is your criteria for choosing materials and finishings in a particular room?
¿Cuál es su criterio a la hora de seleccionar los materiales y los acabados en esta estancia?
Welche Kriterien wenden Sie bei der Entscheidung über Materialen und Oberflächen in diesem Raum an?

1. We do not use specific historic references when designing a residence. We are inspired as much by a Pompeian villa as by a modern house by Neutra or Mies van der Rohe.

2. The location and the requirements are the rational determining factors, while the pursuit of sensibility in the space is our personal approach.

3. The spaces that we consider most interesting are opposites, the most private ones and the ones that are most exposed and public. The former encourage intimacy and contemplation, while the more open living areas are the spatial culmination of the design process.

4. There are several aspects that influence the selection of materials: rational ones like the climate and the availability, and sensory ones like the feeling conveyed by the space.

1. No tenemos referente histórico concreto a la hora de proyectar una vivienda. Para nosotros es igual de inspirador una villa pompeyana que una casa moderna de Neutra o Mies van der Rohe.

2. El lugar y el programa son los factores determinantes racionales, mientras que la búsqueda de la sensibilidad en el espacio se convierte en nuestro objetivo personal.

3. Las estancias que consideramos más interesantes son opuestas: las más íntimas y las más públicas. Las primeras permiten el recogimiento y la contemplación, mientras que las segundas, por ejemplo, las áreas de estar, más abiertas, las entendemos como la conclusión espacial del ejercicio de diseño.

4. Para la selección de un material influyen varios aspectos: los racionales, como el clima y la disponibilidad, y lo sensorial, es decir, lo que el espacio transmite.

1. Wir haben keine konkrete historische Referenz bei der Planung eines Wohnhauses. Uns inspiriert eine pompejische Stadt genauso wie ein modernes Haus von Neutra oder Mies van der Rohe.

2. Der Ort und das Wohnprogramm sind die rationalen Gründe für die Entscheidung, während die Suche nach Sensibilität des Raumes unsere persönliche Suche ist.

3. Die Räume, die wir am interessantesten finden, sind in einer Art Gegenüberstellung die Räume, die am privatesten sind und die, die geteilt und gezeigt werden. In den ersten sucht man die Zurückgezogenheit und die Betrachtung, während in den anderen die Wohnbereiche offener sind. Diese verstehen wie als die räumliche Schlussfolgerung des gestalterischen Eingriffs.

4. Die Materialauswahl wird von verschiedenen Aspekten beeinflusst, rationale Aspekte wie das Klima und die Verfügbarkeit und emotionale Aspekte, die der Raum vermittelt.

Guillermo Arias was born in Bogota, Colombia, and has been an architect at the Universidad de los Andes since 1986. That same year he founded the firm Octubre, where he designs various lighting projects and does architectural work. Since 2002 he has designed lamp collections for Goldsmith in New York.
Luis Cuartas was born in Medellin, Colombia, and has been an architect at the Universidad Javierana since 1990. Since then the two have collaborated on a wide variety of residential and commercial projects.

Guillermo Arias nació en Bogotá, Colombia, y es arquitecto de la Universidad de los Andes desde 1986. En este mismo año fundó la firma Octubre, en donde desarrolla varios proyectos de iluminación paralelamente a su trabajo como arquitecto. Desde 2002 es diseñador de la colección de lámparas para Goldsmith en Nueva York.
Luis Cuartas nació en Medellín, Colombia, y es arquitecto de la Universidad Javeriana desde 1990. Desde entonces, ambos trabajan como arquitectos asociados en una amplia variedad de proyectos residenciales y comerciales.

Guillermo Arias kam in Bogotá in Kolumbien auf die Welt und machte 1986 sein Architekturdiplom an der Universität der Anden. Im gleichen Jahr gründete er das Unternehmen Octubre, in dem er verschiedene Beleuchtungsprojekte parallel zu seiner Arbeit als Architekt verwirklichte. Seit 2002 entwirft er die Lampenkollektion für Goldsmith in New York.
Luis Cuartas wurde in Medellín in Kolumbien geboren und schloss 1990 sein Architekturstudium an der Universität Javeriana ab. Seit diesem Jahr arbeiten die beiden Architekten an zahlreichen Bauprojekten für Wohn- und Geschäftshäuser zusammen.

The clients for this project, a couple with two children, were originally from the Philadelphia area. For the past ten years they have spent their summers on Long Beach Island, an island on the south coast of New Jersey. They were attracted to this property because of its solitary and comfortable character, lent by the area's dense woods. The clients not only wanted to maintain and protect this vegetation, but to make it an integral part of the project so they could enjoy it from within the living areas of the home. These concepts lead to the idea of placing the living quarters of the house on a higher level to create a more direct relationship with the vegetation. The more private areas, like the bedrooms, were placed on an even higher floor, above the trees and with a view of the ocean. The guest room, an office/gym, a storage room, and the building's entrance that faces the woods, are all on the ground floor. A metal framework reinforces the wooden structure and supports the large projections that emphasize the relationship with the surroundings.

Beach House

› Christoff:Finio architecture

Long Beach Island, NY, USA › 2003 › Photos © Elizabeth Felicella

☐ Los clientes de este proyecto, originarios de la zona de Filadelfia, son una pareja con dos hijos. Esta familia ha pasado los veranos de los últimos diez años en Long Beach Island, una isla situada en la costa sur de Nueva Jersey. Adquirieron esta propiedad atraídos por su carácter solitario y acogedor que les confería el denso bosque que existe en el paraje. Los propietarios no sólo querían respetar y proteger esta vegetación, sino integrarla en el

☐ Die Auftraggeber für dieses Haus stammen aus der Gegend von Philadelphia. Es handelt sich um ein Paar mit zwei Kindern, die während der letzten 10 Jahre den Sommer auf Long Beach Island, einer Insel an der Südküste von New Jersey, verbracht haben. Dieses Haus inmitten eines dichten Waldes sagte ihnen aufgrund der zurückgezogenen und gleichzeitig einladenden Lage zu. Die Kunden wollten diesen Wald nicht nur erhalten und

proyecto y poder disfrutarla desde las áreas de estar de la casa. Esta premisa llevó a la idea de plantear las zonas de estar de la vivienda en un nivel más elevado y así tener una relación más directa con la vegetación. La esfera más privada, como las habitaciones, se sitúa en la segunda planta, por encima de la copa de los árboles y con vistas al mar. En la planta baja se ubica la habitación de huéspedes, una oficina-gimnasio, un almacén y el acceso a la vivienda que se abre al bosque. Una estructura metálica tiene como función reforzar la estructura de madera y sustenta los voladizos que ensalzan la relación con el entorno.

beschützen, sondern ihn auch zu einem integralen Bestandteil der Planung machen, und ihn vom Wohnzimmer des Hauses aus genießen. Dadurch kam den Planern die Idee, die Wohnbereiche des Hauses auf einer etwas höheren Ebene anzulegen, um so eine direkte Beziehung zur Vegetation zu haben. Die privateren Räume wie die Schlafzimmer liegen auf einer noch höheren Ebene, über den Bäumen und mit Blick aufs Meer. Im Erdgeschoss befinden sich das Gästezimmer, ein Büro-Fitnessraum, ein Lager und der Zugang zum Haus, der sich zum Wald hin öffnet. Eine Metallstruktur verstärkt die Holzstruktur und stützt die großen Vorsprünge, die Beziehung zur Umgebung unterstreichen.

0 2 4

› Ground floor
› Planta baja
› Erdegeschoss

› First floor
› Planta primera
› Erster Stock

› Second floor
› Planta segunda
› Zweiter Stock

0   2   4

> Sections

> Secciones

> Schnitte

1. What historical reference in particular inspires you when designing a residence?
¿Qué referente histórico en particular le sirve de fuente de inspiración a la hora de proyectar una vivienda?
Welche historische Referenz dient Ihnen als Inspiration beim Entwurf eines Hauses?

2. What is the main factor taken into consideration when designing a residence?
¿Cuál es el principal factor determinante a la hora de diseñar una vivienda?
Welche Rahmenbedingungen, bzw. Faktoren sind für Sie ausschlaggebend beim Konzipieren?

3. What room inside the home do you find most interesting to design?
¿Qué estancia de la vivienda encuentra usted más interesante para diseñar?
Welchen Raum des Hauses finden Sie am spannendsten zu entwerfen?

4. What is your criteria for choosing materials and finishings in a particular room?
¿Cuál es su criterio a la hora de seleccionar los materiales y los acabados en esta estancia?
Welche Kriterien wenden Sie bei der Entscheidung über Materialen und Oberflächen in diesem Raum an?

1. The history of domesticity.

2. How to dignify living.

3. Any room that can extend outdoors.

4. Quiet innovation.

1. La historia de lo doméstico.

2. Cómo ampliar una vivienda.

3. Cualquier habitación que se abra al exterior.

4. La innovación moderada.

1. Die Geschichte der Häuslichkeit.

2. Wie kann man eine Wohnung vergrößern.

3. Alle Räume, die sich nach außen öffnen.

4. Die maßvolle Innovation.

Martin Finio graduated from Cooper Union in New York. For ten years he was an associate architect in the office of Tod Williams and Billie Tsien, where he lead and participated in a wide variety of projects. He was the editor of the monograph "William Tsien: Works", and was a professor at Columbia and Yale Universities.
Taryn Christoff graduated from IIT and worked for several years in New York on large and small-scale projects, gaining experience in both corporate and residential projects. She founded the firm which Martin Finio would later join to create Christoff:Finio architecture.

Martin Finio se graduó en la Cooper Union de Nueva York y fue arquitecto asociado durante diez años en la oficina de Tod Williams y Billie Tsien, en donde lideró y participó en una amplia variedad de proyectos. Ha trabajado como editor en la monografía "William Tsien: Works" así como de profesor en las universidades de Columbia y Yale.
Taryn Christoff se graduó en IIT y trabajó durante varios años en Nueva York en proyectos de gran y pequeña escala ganando experiencia tanto en proyectos corporativos como residenciales. Fundó la firma a la que más tarde se incorporó Martin Finio para crear Christoff:Finio architecture.

Martin Finio studierte an der Cooper Union in New York ab und war 10 Jahre lang als assoziierter Architekt bei Tod Williams und Billie Tsien tätig, wo er an einer großen Reihe an Projekten teilnahm oder sie leitete. Er arbeitete als Herausgeber der Monographie „William Tsien: Works" und als Professor an den Universitäten von Columbia und Yale. Taryn Christoff schloss seine Studien an der IIT ab und arbeitete mehrere Jahre in New York, wo er Erfahrungen sowohl bei der Planung von Geschäfts- als auch Wohnhäusern sammelte. Er gründete die Firma, der später auch Martin Finio beitrat, und aus der dann Christoff:Finio architecture entstand.

□ This wood house, located in a rural area where stone is the principal construction material, was inspired by the agricultural buildings of the region. The architect defines the project as a granary for an artist, because the house incorporates a working studio. The goal was to capture the best views of Lake Maggiore, so the building was designed in the form of a tower that was predominately vertical. The structural walls are made of concrete, while the interior walls are fabricated from insulated panels that are lighter and more flexible. The covering on the exterior, composed of narrow wood boards, emphasizes the verticality of the building even more, while a balcony that faces the west acts as a horizontal counterpoint. The location on the highest part of a hill represented a construction challenge, because there was no existing entrance from the highway. As a result of this the architects chose a prefabricated wood structure that was assembled in three days with the help of a helicopter.

Casa Larga

› Daniele Claudio Taddei

Kloten, Switzerland › 2001 › Photos © Bruno Helbling / zapaimages

☐ Ubicada en una zona rural, en donde se emplea principalmente la piedra como material de construcción, esta casa de madera se inspira en las construcciones agrícolas de la región. El arquitecto define el proyecto como un granero para un artista, ya que se trata de una vivienda que incorpora un estudio de trabajo. La premisa del proyecto era la de alcanzar las mejores panorámicas del lago Maggiore, por lo que el volumen se plantea como un

☐ Dieses Holzhaus, das in einem ländlichen Gebiet liegt, in dem hauptsächlich Steine als Baumaterial verwendet werden, ist von den Bauernhäusern der Region inspiriert. Der Architekt definiert das Gebäude als eine Scheune für einen Künstler, da es sich um ein Wohnhaus mit einem Atelier handelt. Von dem Gebäude aus sollte man einen der besten Panoramablicke auf den Lago Maggiore genießen, deshalb ist es vertikal wie ein Turm aufgebaut. Die

elemento vertical, en forma de torre. Los muros estructurales están construidos de hormigón, mientras que los tabiques que dividen el interior están fabricados con paneles aislantes y permiten una mayor flexibilidad y ligereza. El revestimiento exterior de la fachada, a partir de listones de madera, ensalzan aún más la verticalidad del edificio, mientras que un balcón mirador orientado hacia el oeste, sirve de contrapunto horizontal. El emplazamiento, en la cima de una colina, representó un desafío constructivo, ya que no existía acceso desde la carretera. En consecuencia, recurrieron a un sistema prefabricado de madera que se montó en tres días con la ayuda de un helicóptero.

tragenden Wände sind aus Beton, während die Zwischenwände im Inneren aus Isolierpaneelen sind, was die Gestaltung flexibler macht und dem Haus mehr Leichtigkeit verleiht. Die Fassade ist von außen mit Holzlatten verkleidet, was die vertikale Form noch unterstreicht. Ein Aussichtsbalkon mit Blick nach Westen dient als horizontaler Kontrapunkt. Der Standort oben auf einem Hügel war eine Herausforderung für die Planer, da es keine Zufahrt von der Landstraße aus gibt. Deshalb wurde das Gebäude mit einem Fertighaussystem aus Holz errichtet, das mit einem Hubschrauber transportiert und in drei Tagen montiert wurde.

0 1 2

› **Ground floor**

› Planta baja

› Erdegeschoss

› **First floor**

› Planta primera

› Erster Stock

› **Second floor**

› Planta segunda

› Zweiter Stock

› **Sections**
› Secciones
› Schnitt

› **Elevation**
› Alzado
› Aufriss

0 1 2

Daniele Claudio Taddei was born in Lugano, Switzerland, in 1960. He pursued his early studies in Lugano and Tarasp, Switzerland, and continued with advanced studies in Stuttgart, Germany, graduating in 1986. He worked as an architect in several offices in Germany, Italy, the United States, and Switzerland. Since 2001 he has his own firm in Zurich, where he designs a variety of architecture and interior projects.

Daniele Claudio Taddei nació en Lugano, Suiza, en 1960. Después de cursar sus primeros estudios en Lugano y Tarasp, Suiza, continuó sus estudios superiores en Stuttgart, Alemania, en donde se graduó en 1986. Ha trabajado como arquitecto colaborador en varias oficinas de Alemania, Italia, Estados Unidos y Suiza. A partir de 2001 funda su propia firma en Zurich, en donde desarrolla una gran variedad de proyectos de arquitectura y diseño interior.

Daniele Claudio Taddei kam 1960 in Lugan in der Schweiz auf die Welt. Nachdem er sein Studium in Lugan und Tarasp in der Schweiz begonnen hatte, setzte er es in Stuttgart in Deutschland fort, wo er 1986 sein Diplom erwarb. Er arbeitete als Architekt mit verschiedenen Architekturbüros in Deutschland, Italien, in den Vereinigten Staaten und in der Schweiz zusammen. Im Jahre 2001 gründete er seine eigene Firma in Zürich, mit der er eine Vielzahl von Projekten in den Bereichen Architektur und Innenarchitektur durchführt.

□ The main challenge of this project was designing a house that would take full advantage of the many views, while maintaining the privacy of its occupants and blending in with the surrounding environment. One part of the property faces the Andes mountain range including Cotopaxi, the highest snow-covered active volcano in Ecuador. The architects Wood + Zapata designed a house that was adapted to the site's mountainous terrain. The two main wings of the building form a large angle, allowing them to take in most of the views and create a feeling of proximity. A projecting terrace on the main wing of the house extends from the dining room towards Cotopaxi. The other wing ends at a road that borders the mountain and the swimming pool, which also extends outwards from inside the building. The façade that faces the mountain is almost entirely covered with green-colored glass, so one can always enjoy the view from the inside. From the outside the house blends into the landscape when viewed from across the valley.

House in Miravalle

› Wood + Zapata

Miravalle, Ecuador › 2002 › Photos © Undine Pröhl

☐ El mayor reto de este proyecto consistía en diseñar una casa que aprovechara las múltiples ventajas visuales del entorno, pero al mismo tiempo mantuviera la intimidad de sus habitantes y se adaptara al paisaje circundante. Una parte del solar se orienta hacia la cordillera de los Andes con Cotopaxi, el volcán activo nevado de más altitud en Ecuador. Los arquitectos Wood + Zapata diseñaron la vivienda para que se adaptara a la naturaleza

☐ Die große Herausforderung bei dieser Planung war es, ein Haus zu entwerfen, das die interessante Aussicht integriert, aber gleichzeitig die Privatsphäre der Bewohner schützt und sich der Umgebung anpasst. Von einer Seite des Grundstückes sieht man auf die Andenkette und den Cotopaxi, den höchsten aktiven Vulkan in Ecuador. Die Architekten Wood + Zapata haben das Haus an die bergige Landschaft angepasst. Die beiden Hauptflügel des

montañosa del lugar. Las dos alas principales del proyecto plantean un amplio ángulo entre ellas y de este modo abarcan la mayor parte de las vistas y se acercan más a ellas. El ala principal de la casa alberga una terraza en voladizo que se extiende a partir del comedor en eje hacia el Cotopaxi. La otra ala finaliza en un camino que bordea la montaña y en la piscina que se prolonga también desde el interior de la vivienda. La fachada que mira hacia la montaña está casi totalmente revestida de un cristal coloreado de verde, que permite disfrutar permanentemente de las vistas panorámicas; desde el otro lado del valle, el exterior de la casa es visto como parte integrante del paisaje.

Gebäudes bilden einen weiten Winkel, um die wundervolle Aussicht näher zu bringen und so weit wie möglich zu umfassen. Der Hauptflügel des Hauses läuft in eine Terrasse auf einem Vorsprung aus, der sich vom Esszimmer in der Achse bis zum Cotopaxi erstreckt. Der andere Flügel endet an einem Weg, der an dem Berg entlang führt und am Swimmingpool, der ebenfalls bis in das Innere des Hauses reicht. Die Fassade zum Berg hin besteht fast vollständig aus grünem Glas, so dass man vom Inneren aus ständig diesen überwältigenden Blick hat und von außen, von der anderen Seite des Tales aus betrachtet, verschwindet das Haus fast in der Landschaft.

› **Ground floor**
› Planta baja
› Erdegeschoss

› **First floor**
› Planta primera
› Erster Stock

› Elevations

› Alzados

› Aufriss

› Section

› Sección

› Schnitt

1. What historical reference in particular inspires you when designing a residence?
¿Qué referente histórico en particular le sirve de fuente de inspiración a la hora de proyectar una vivienda?
Welche historische Referenz dient Ihnen als Inspiration beim Entwurf eines Hauses?

2. What is the main factor taken into consideration when designing a residence?
¿Cuál es el principal factor determinante a la hora de diseñar una vivienda?
Welche Rahmenbedingungen, bzw. Faktoren sind für Sie ausschlaggebend beim Konzipieren?

3. What room inside the home do you find most interesting to design?
¿Qué estancia de la vivienda encuentra usted más interesante para diseñar?
Welchen Raum des Hauses finden Sie am spannendsten zu entwerfen?

4. What is your criteria for choosing materials and finishings in a particular room?
¿Cuál es su criterio a la hora de seleccionar los materiales y los acabados en esta estancia?
Welche Kriterien wenden Sie bei der Entscheidung über Materialen und Oberflächen in diesem Raum an?

1. There is no particular reference that applies to all residence projects. Obviously, there are masterfully executed houses that are part of the knowledge of every architect, such as the Schindler House, Falling Water, and works by Lautner, however, it is important to reconize the importance that the site has on the particular work.

2. Obviously the client. A custom designed residence should reflect the lifestyle of the person or family who commissions it. Equally important is the site and the climate in which it's built.

3. Each room is an element that completes the composition of the house. It's hard for me to pick one.

4. I use materials as providing color and texture as well as defining relationships between planes, however, in a house or room it is most important to create a warm balance between all the materials.

1. No hay una referencia concreta aplicable a todos los proyectos residenciales. Obviamente, hay casas magistralmente diseñadas que están en la mente de todo arquitecto, como la casa Schindler, la casa de la Cascada y los trabajos de Lautner; sin embargo, es importante reconocer la relevancia que tiene el emplazamiento dentro de un trabajo concreto.

2. El cliente, obviamente. Una casa debe reflejar el estilo de vida de la persona o la familia que encarga el proyecto; es igual de importante el lugar y el clima donde se emplaza.

3. Cada habitación es un elemento que complementa la composición de la casa. Es difícil escoger una.

4. Utilizo materiales que proporcionen color y textura y que definan las relaciones entre los planos; sin embrago, en una casa o una estancia lo más importante es crear un cálido equilibrio entre todos los materiales.

1. Es gibt keine konkrete Referenz, die man auf alle Wohnprojekte anwenden kann. Offensichtlich gibt es perfekt geplante Häuser, an die jeder Architekt denkt, wie das Haus Schindler, und das Haus Wasserfall die Arbeiten von Lautner, dennoch ist es wichtig, an die Bedeutung des Standortes für eine konkrete Planung zu denken.

2. Natürlich der Kunde. Ein Haus sollte den Lebensstil einer Person oder einer Familie, die es sich bauen lässt, widerspiegeln. Das ist ebenso wichtig wie der Standort und das Klima der Umgebung.

3. Jeder Raum ist ein Element, das die Gestaltung des Hauses beeinflusst. Es ist schwierig, einen auszuwählen.

4. Ich benutze Materialien, die Farbe und Textur besitzen und die die Beziehungen zwischen den Ebenen definieren. Dennoch ist es in einem Haus oder einer Wohnung wichtig, ein warmes Gleichgewicht zwischen allen Materialien zu schaffen.

Since its inception in 1996, Wood + Zapata has made an effort to imprint its personal design perspective on each of the many different projects it has completed. These include the Chicago Bears Stadium, several private homes, spaces for commercial use, large-scale residential complexes, the new international terminal at the Miami airport, and the new construction and total rehabilitation of two blocks of the French historic center in Shanghai. From their offices in New York and Shanghai, they work on projects that range from master plans to furniture design.

Desde sus inicios en 1996, la firma Wood + Zapata se ha esforzado por impregnar su personal perspectiva del diseño en cada uno de los variados proyectos que han ejecutado. Entre sus obras se encuentran el estadio Chicago Bears, numerosas casas privadas, proyectos de uso comercial, complejos residenciales de gran escala, la nueva terminal internacional del aeropuerto de Miami y la completa rehabilitación y nueva construcción de dos bloques del centro histórico francés de Shangai. En sus dos oficinas, en Nueva York y Shangai, desarrollan proyectos que comprenden desde planes maestros hasta el diseño de mobiliario.

Seit der Gründung 1996 hat die Firma Wood + Zapata sich stets darum bemüht, ihre persönliche, architektonische Perspektive in jede ihrer Planungen einzubringen. Zu ihren Arbeiten gehören das Chicago Bears Stadium, viele Privat- und Geschäftshäuser, große Wohnkomplexe, das neue, internationale Terminal am Flughafen von Miami und der völlige Um- und Neubau von zwei Häuserblöcken im historischen, französischen Viertel von Shanghai. In ihren Büros in New York und Shanghai entwickeln sie Projekte, die von Masterplänen bis hin zum Möbeldesign reichen.

□ This house replaced one of the many modern homes built in the 1950's in Portola Valley, California. The neighborhood is characterized by well-groomed landscaping, a comfortable distance between buildings, and green areas that incorporate many walking trails. It was developed following the conventional notion of what constituted modern living during the middle of the last century. The architects were faced with the creation of a design that would fit in with the older existing environment and at the same time embody contemporary ideals. The clients, for their part, wanted a home that would incorporate attractive work areas. The design of the house, therefore, had to focus on both the public areas and those used for business meetings. The architects' response to these requirements was to articulate the public spaces, located on the lower level, and the private spaces in the upper floor, which are turned opposite those of the lower level to take enjoy the view of the valley. The composition is based on a series of long, brightly colored walls that extend across the lot, with a few transversal planes that create a series of rooms that fulfill the requirements of the internal functions.

Castor Packard House

› Callas Shortridge Architects

Portola Valley, CA, USA › 2002 › Photos © Tim Griffith

☐ Esta casa reemplaza una de las muchas viviendas modernas construidas en la década de 1950 en Portola Valley, California. Este barrio se caracteriza por un paisaje cuidado, que mantiene cierta distancia entre las edificaciones y conserva numerosos senderos peatonales vinculados a las zonas de vegetación. En este entorno, creado con las nociones convencionales del concepto de vida moderna de mediados de siglo pasado, los arquitectos

☐ Dieses Haus befindet sich dort, wo eines der zahlreichen, modernen Wohnhäuser aus den Fünfzigerjahren in Portola Valley, Kalifornien stand. Das Viertel zeichnet sich durch eine gepflegte Landschaft und einen relativ großen Abstand zwischen den einzelnen Häusern aus. Es gibt viele kleine Fußwege, die in die Natur führen. In dieser Umgebung, die nach den konventionellen Gesichtspunkten des modernen Lebens Mitte des vergangenen

estaban ante un proyecto que debían conciliar características del pasado y al mismo tiempo un paisaje contemporáneo. Los clientes, por su parte, querían una vivienda que incorporara zonas de trabajo acogedoras. El diseño de la casa debía entonces destacar en las áreas públicas y de reuniones laborales. El desarrollo del proyecto se basa en la solución arquitectónica para articular los espacios públicos, ubicados en la planta baja, y los espacios privados, concentrados en un volumen superior con diferente orientación que el inferior para aprovechar las panorámicas del valle. La composición se centra en una serie de muros estructurales longitudinales de colores vivos que se extienden a lo largo del solar, mientras que ciertos planos transversales crean una secuencia de estancias que solucionan el programa de funciones internas.

Jahrhunderts entstanden ist, standen die Architekten vor der Herausforderung, ein Gebäude zu schaffen, das mit der Vergangenheit im Dialog steht und gleichzeitig die Kennzeichen der zeitgenössischen Landschaft aufweist. Die Kunden wünschten sich ein Wohnhaus mit komfortablen Arbeitsbereichen. Es mussten also öffentliche Bereiche und Orte für professionelle Zusammenkünfte geschaffen werden. Das Gebäude wurde so angelegt, dass sich die öffentlich genutzten Räume im Erdgeschoss und die privaten Wohnräume im Obergeschoss befinden, und zwar nach hinten, um den Panoramablick auf das Tal zu integrieren. Die Gestaltung wird durch eine Reihe von strukturellen, längs verlaufenden Wänden in lebendigen Farben geprägt, die am ganzen Grundstück entlang führen, während bestimmte quer verlaufende Ebenen Sequenzen von Räumen sind, die für verschiedene Funktionen bestimmt sind.

› **Elevations**
› Alzados
› Aufrisse

› **Ground floor**
› Planta baja
› Erdgeschoss

› **First floor**
› Planta primera
› Erster Stock

> Sections
> Secciones
> Schnitte

0 4 8

The architectural firm of Callas Shortridge Architects has been in existence since 1996. Their founders, Steven Shortridge and Barbara Callas were architects at Israel Design Associates of Beverly Hills. Before starting their own office, the two worked together as project architects on a wide range of assignments of different scales. Barbara heads the development of projects that require detailed technical knowledge. Steven leads and manages the design and construction process for the firm's different projects. Both have received many prestigious awards for their design work.

La firma Callas Shortridge Architects existe desde 1996. Sus fundadores, Steven Shortridge y Barbara Callas formaron parte como arquitectos asociados de la firma Israel Design Associates, en Beverly Hills. Antes de crear su propia oficina, ambos colaboraron como arquitectos proyectistas desarrollando una amplia variedad de trabajos de diferentes escalas. Barbara lidera el desarrollo de proyectos, lo cuales requieren profundos conocimientos técnicos. Steven dirige y maneja el proceso de diseño y construcción para los diferentes proyectos de la firma. Ambos han recibido numeros premios prestigiosos de diseño por su trabajo.

Callas Shortridge Architects existiert seit dem Jahr 1996. Die Gründer Steven Shortridge und Barbara Callas waren vorher als assoziierte Architekten bei Israel Design Associates in Beverly Hills tätig. Bevor sie ihr eigenes Architekturbüro ins Leben riefen, arbeiteten sie als Projektarchitekten an Planungen verschiedener Größenordnung mit. Barbara überwacht die Projektabwicklung bei Planungen, für die ausgezeichnete technische Kenntnisse notwendig sind. Steven leitet den Gestaltungs- und Bauprozess für die veschiedenen Projekte des Unternehmens. Beide erhielten für ihr Werk bereits wichtige Designpreise.

☐ This house is located in a suburb of the area of Boston, an area known for its low hills and a wide variety of residential construction. The clients are an older couple whose children no longer live with them, and they wanted a comfortable, functional, and adaptable home for their retirement. The wife's professional dedication to cooking largely determined the configuration of the residence and the importance of this activity within the house. The essential parameters of the design plan were dealing with the elongated shape of the property in combination with the steep angle of the terrain, the pursuit of views, and the difficulty of creating an access for vehicles. The resulting building has two levels; the bedrooms are located on the ground floor, and the main living space occupies the upper floor, which has the best views of the area. A functional look was given to the front elevation of the building that at the same time incorporates the symbolic and utilitarian presence of the automobile.

May Residence

› Jonathan Levi Architects

Brookline, MA, USA › 1996 › Photos © Anton Grassl / Jonathan Levi Architects

☐ Esta vivienda se emplaza en un suburbio del área de Boston, una zona caracterizada por suaves colinas y una amplia variedad de construcciones residenciales. Los clientes son una pareja de la tercera edad cuyos hijos han crecido y viven fuera de casa, por lo que querían una confortable, funcional y adaptable vivienda de retiro. La dedicación profesional de la esposa a la cocina determinó en gran medida la configuración de la vivienda y la

☐ Dieses Haus befindet sich in der Vorstadt von Boston in einer Region mit sanften Hügelketten und zahlreichen Wohnhäusern. Die Kunden sind ein älteres Paar mit erwachsenen Kindern, die nicht mehr zuhause wohnen. Sie wünschten sich eine komfortable, funktionelle und nicht allzu große Wohnung für ihren Lebensabend. Da die Dame des Hauses sich beruflich dem Kochen widmet, spielt die Küche innerhalb der Struktur des Hauses eine

importancia de este espacio dentro de ella. El principal punto de partida en el diseño del proyecto era resolver la forma alargada del solar con el desnivel del terreno, la búsqueda de visuales y la dificultad para crear el acceso del vehículo. El volumen se soluciona en dos plantas. En la planta baja se ubican las habitaciones, mientras que el área principal de estar se sitúa en el nivel superior para poder disfrutar de las mejores panorámicas de la zona. Se buscó crear una imagen doméstica para el alzado frontal, pero que al mismo tiempo incorporara la presencia simbólica y funcional del automóvil.

große Rolle. Der Ausgangspunkt der Planung war es, eine Lösung für die relativ schwierige, längliche Form des Geländes mit starker Neigung zu finden, visuelle Höhepunkte und eine Zufahrt für Fahrzeuge zu schaffen. Das Gebäude besteht aus zwei Stockwerken, im Erdgeschoss befinden sich die Schlafzimmer und im Obergeschoss das Wohnzimmer, von dem aus man den besten Blick hat. Man versuchte, die Vorderfront einladend und wohnlich wirken zu lassen, aber gleichzeitig dort auch die symbolische und funktionelle Präsenz des Autos zu integrieren.

0 2 4

› Roof plan

› Planta de cubiertas

› Dachgrundriss

› First floor

› Planta primera

› Erster Stock

› Second floor

› Planta segunda

› Zweiter Stock

› Transversal sections

› Secciones transversales

› Querschnitte

› Longitudinal section

› Sección longitudinal

› Längaufriss

0   2   4

Jonathan Levi Architects is an architecture and interior design firm. Their buildings and interior spaces support and reinforce the highest aspirations of their clients. Their source of inspiration for every project stems from a comprehensive study of the conditions surrounding the individual project, and the close collaboration of the client. A rigorous design method based on the exploration of different alternatives guides their response to each design challenge. This results in conceptual clarity and the responsible use of resources.

Jonathan Levi Architects es una firma de arquitectura y diseño interior que se encarga de que los edificios y los espacios interiores cumplan las máximas aspiraciones de sus clientes. En cada obra se toma como fuente de inspiración la estrecha colaboración con el cliente y una exhaustiva investigación de las condiciones que envuelven cada proyecto. La respuesta a cada situación viene dada por un riguroso método de diseño organizado a partir de la comprobación de diferentes alternativas. El resultado se traduce en una economía de medios y en una claridad conceptual.

Jonathan Levi Architects ist ein Architektur- und Innenarchitekturstudio, das Gebäude und Innenräume plant, die den Wünschen und Bedürfnissen ihrer Kunden so weit wie möglich gerecht werden. Bei jeder dieser Planungen ist die Inspirationsquelle die enge Zusammenarbeit mit dem Kunden und eine genaue Analyse der Bedingungen jedes einzelnen Bauvorhabens. Die Antwort auf jede Situation entsteht aus der strengen und organisierten Planung der Gestaltung nach Überprüfung mehrerer Alternativen. So entstehen Gebäude mit niedrigen Kosten und einem klaren Konzept.

☐ The C-House is a small yet complex urban building that is used for two different purposes: a residential studio and a commercial café, both of which belong to the same client. The place is on the outskirts of Tokyo, and it presented a difficult challenge because two major streets with heavy traffic surround the site. Rather than a simple juxtaposition of functions, combining the two designs was simply a reflection of Tokyo's contemporary urban lifestyle. Nowadays the private life of a resident of this city directly depends on the conditions of the city's public spaces. The line between what is private and what is public is becoming progressively blurred. The C-House is, therefore, an architectural materialization of this reality, and could be seen as a representation of the urban prototype in a single building. The transparent rooms of the café, located on the lower level and the terrace, literally wrap around the opaque volume that houses the private functions of the residence. The two sections of the project have independent access from the street, but at the same time they are connected internally, which emphasizes the flow between the two areas.

C-House

› Toshimitsu Kuno, Nobuki Nomura / tele-design

Tokyo, Japan › 2002 › Photos © Tatsuya Noaki, Tamotsu Matsumoto

☐ La casa C es un edificio pequeño, pero al mismo tiempo complejo que acomoda dos programas urbanos diferentes: un estudio residencial y un café comercial, ambos propiedad del mismo cliente. El lugar se encuentra a las afueras de Tokio y presenta una situación compleja, ya que dos carreteras importantes y de continuo tráfico delimitan el solar. La conjunción de los dos programas, más que una simple yuxtaposición de las funciones, es

☐ Das Haus – C ist ein kleines, aber gleichzeitig sehr komplexes Gebäude, das zwei verschiedenen Zwecken dient, zum einen ist es ein Wohnatelier und zum anderen ein Café. Beide gehören dem Kunden selbst. Der Grundstück liegt am Stadtrand von Tokio und relativ ungünstig, da es von zwei viel befahrenen Straßen begrenzt wird. Diese Kombination zweier Funktionen, die nicht einfach nur in einem Nebeneinanderstellen besteht,

simplemente un reflejo de la vida urbana contemporánea de Tokio. En la actualidad, la intimidad de un individuo en esta ciudad se convierte en una dependencia directa de las condiciones del espacio público de la urbe. Los límites entre la esfera privada y pública cada vez son más inestables, borrosos e incluso temporales. La casa C se convierte entonces en la materialización arquitectónica de esta realidad que deriva en lo que se podría entender como prototipo urbano en un solo edificio. Las salas transparentes del café, ubicadas en la planta baja y el terrado, envuelven literalmente el volumen opaco que contiene las funciones del ámbito privado de la vivienda. Las dos partes del programa disponen de accesos independientes desde la calle, pero al mismo tiempo se comunican internamente acentuando la fluidez entre las dos zonas.

ist lediglich eine Widerspiegelung des gegenwärtigen städtischen Lebens in Tokio. Das Privatleben eines Individuums in dieser Stadt hängt im steigenden Maße von den Bedingungen der öffentlichen Räume der Stadt ab. Die Grenzen zwischen privat und öffentlich werden immer instabiler, verwischter und sogar vorübergehend. Das Haus – C ist also die architektonische Materialisierung dieser Wirklichkeit und wird so zu einer Art urbaner Prototyp in einem einzigen Gebäude. Die transparenten Teile des Cafés im Erdgeschoss und das Flachdach umgeben die undurchsichtigen Gebäudeteile, in denen die Privaträume des Hauses liegen. Für beide Bereiche gibt es unabhängige Zugänge von der Straße aus, aber gleichzeitig sind sie miteinander verbunden, was den fließenden Übergang zwischen beiden Zonen noch unterstreicht.

0 2 4

› **Ground floor**
› Planta baja
› Erdegeschoss

› **First floor**
› Planta primera
› Erster Stock

› **Second floor**
› Planta segunda
› Zweiter Stock

› **Longitudinal section**
› Sección longitudinal
› Längaufriss

› **Transversal section**
› Sección transversal
› Querschnitt

diagram-plan

diagram-section

› Axonometry
› Axonometría
› Axonometrie

› Diagrams
› Esquemas
› Schema

1. What historical reference in particular inspires you when designing a residence?
   ¿Qué referente histórico en particular le sirve de fuente de inspiración a la hora de proyectar una vivienda?
   Welche historische Referenz dient Ihnen als Inspiration beim Entwurf eines Hauses?

2. What is the main factor taken into consideration when designing a residence?
   ¿Cuál es el principal factor determinante a la hora de diseñar una vivienda?
   Welche Rahmenbedingungen, bzw. Faktoren sind für Sie ausschlaggebend beim Konzipieren?

3. What room inside the home do you find most interesting to design?
   ¿Qué estancia de la vivienda encuentra usted más interesante para diseñar?
   Welchen Raum des Hauses finden Sie am spannendsten zu entwerfen?

4. What is your criteria for choosing materials and finishings in a particular room?
   ¿Cuál es su criterio a la hora de seleccionar los materiales y los acabados en esta estancia?
   Welche Kriterien wenden Sie bei der Entscheidung über Materialen und Oberflächen in diesem Raum an?

1. We explore flexible and transitive spatial condition in response to owners' needs. We try to understand the character of site as much as possible and then make it reflect on the positioning and composition of the residential space.

2. We don't design too much and try to leave the space or condition into which the owners can intervene spontaneously.

3. Communal space such as living, dinning and kitchen, because such space causes various interaction among the family.

4. We make an effort to transform the owners' requests into appropriate materials in a specific and precise manner.

1. Exploramos las condiciones de flexibilidad y transición del espacio en respuesta a las necesidades del propietario. Intentamos entender lo mejor posible las características del lugar para después reflejarlas en la situación y composición del espacio residencial.

2. No diseñamos demasiado, procuramos dejar el espacio en unas condiciones en las que los propietarios puedan intervenir espontáneamente.

3. Los espacios públicos, como la sala de estar, el comedor y la cocina, porque estos espacios promueven la interacción entre la familia.

4. Hacemos un esfuerzo para transformar las necesidades del propietario en los materiales adecuados de un modo preciso y específico.

1. Wir erforschen die Bedingungen der Flexibilität und des Übergangs des Raumes und versuchen damit, den Bedürfnissen des Eigentümers zu entsprechen. Wir versuchen, die Eigentümlichkeiten des Ortes so gut wie möglich zu verstehen, um sie dann in der Lage und Anordnung des Wohnhauses oder der Wohnung widerzuspiegeln.

2. Wir greifen zurückhaltend ein. Wir möchten den Raum so lassen, dass auch die Eigentümer spontane Eingriffe vornehmen können.

3. Die von allen genutzten Räume wie das Wohnzimmer, das Esszimmer und die Küche, da es die Räume sind, in denen das Familienleben stattfindet.

4. Wir versuchen, die geeigneten Materialien präzise und spezifisch für die Bedürfnisse des Kunden auszuwählen.

Tele-design was established with the purpose of incorporating two important tendencies of contemporary Japanese society into the vision and structure of the company. The first was the pursuit of new models of economic growth, and the second was the rapid development of telecommunications within the global economy. In this way design becomes a tool for exploration as well as a vehicle for the incorporation of the latest technologies. Tele-design consists of a multi-disciplinary team that has worked together since 1999. Its unique structure has caught the attention of clients, the press and international critics.

Tele-design se estableció con ánimo de incorporar dos tendencias significativas de la actual sociedad japonesa en la visión y estructura de la compañía. En primer lugar, la búsqueda de nuevos modelos tras el crecimiento económico y en segundo lugar, el rápido desarrollo de las telecomunicaciones en la economía global. De esta manera, el diseño se convierte en una herramienta para explorar y nutrirse de las últimas tecnologías. Por este motivo, tele-design está formado por un equipo pluridisciplinar que colabora junto desde 1999. Su particular estructura ha llamado la atención no sólo de clientes, sino de la prensa y la crítica internacional.

Tele-design wurde gegründet, um zwei wichtige Tendenzen der heutigen japanischen Gesellschaft in die Unternehmensstruktur zu integrieren. Diese Tendenzen sind die Suche nach neuen Modellen nach dem starken Wirtschaftswachstum und die schnelle Entwicklung der Telekommunikationen in der globalen Wirtschaft. So wurde das Design zu einem Werkzeug, um die neusten Technologien zu erforschen und sich von ihnen zu nähren. Tele-design arbeitet daher seit 1999 mit einem multidisziplinäres Team. Diese besondere Struktur erweckte viel Aufmerksamkeit seitens der Kunden und der internationalen Presse und Kritik.

☐ This house is located in Mt. Washington, a diverse neighborhood sitting on the rolling hills very near the center of Los Angeles. Designed as a residence for the architects themselves, it is constructed around a concrete and steel modular framework. They conceived the house as a flexible and expandable environment that would evolve according to their future requirements. The most important considerations of the design were natural light, the connections between the spaces, and the relationship between the interior and the exterior. Both the budget and conservation of the natural environment were important considerations.

The project was optimized by constructing only what was necessary. The outdoor areas of this house were treated as extensions of the interior spaces, the traffic areas fulfill a double function, and the garage and attic were designed to house other functions in the future. By making full use of the possible extensions towards the outdoors and reducing the unused space to a minimum they achieved a modestly sized yet functional building. The interior design of the house was based on the relationships between the spaces, which were emphasized with bright and contrasting colors.

Fung + Blatt House

› Fung + Blatt Architects

Los Angeles, CA, USA › 2003 › Photos © Deborah Bird

☐ La casa se erige en Mt. Washington, un barrio heterogéneo asentado en suaves colinas próximas al centro de Los Ángeles. La vivienda, diseñada como residencia para los propios arquitectos, está construida alrededor de una armadura modular de hormigón y acero. Concibieron su casa como un entorno flexible y expansible que evolucionara con sus futuras necesidades. La luz natural, las conexiones espaciales y la relación entre interior y

☐ Das Haus befindet sich in Mt. Washington in einem sehr vielseitigen Stadtteil zwischen sanften Hügeln ganz in der Nähe vom Zentrum Los Angeles. Das Wohnhaus wurde von den Architekten selbst entworfen und umgibt ein modulares Grundgerippe aus Beton und Stahl. Sie entwarfen ihr Haus als eine flexible und dehnbare Umgebung, die sich mit den zukünftigen Bedürfnissen weiterentwickeln kann. Das Tageslicht, die Verbindungen

exterior fueron consideraciones primordiales en el diseño. Tanto el presupuesto como la conservación ambiental han sido, asimismo, consideraciones prácticas que tener en cuenta. Se optimizó al máximo el proyecto al construir tan solo lo necesario. En esta casa, las zonas exteriores son prolongaciones del espacio interior, las áreas de circulación cumplen una doble función y los volúmenes del garaje y el ático están planteados para albergar otro tipo de labores en un futuro. Al maximizar las posibles extensiones hacia el exterior y al reducir al mínimo el espacio inútil se logró un volumen modesto y al mismo tiempo funcional. Formalmente, la casa se resuelve por medio de un rico juego de volúmenes acentuado por los contrastes y los colores intensos.

zwischen den Räumen und die Beziehung zwischen außen und innen spielten eine besonders große Rolle bei der Planung. Andere praktische Überlegungen mit gleichem Stellenwert sind die Kosten und der behutsame Umgang mit der Umwelt. Deshalb wurde die Planung optimiert, indem nur das wirklich Notwendige gebaut wurde. In diesem Haus sind die Außenbereiche eine Verlängerung der Innenräume, die Flure und Wege erfüllen eine doppelte Funktion und die Garage und der Dachraum sind so ausgelegt, dass sie in der Zukunft auch anderen Zwecken dienen können. Durch die Maximierung der Erweiterungen nach außen und Minimierung des nicht genutzten Raumes entstand ein Gebäude, das bescheiden und gleichzeitig sehr funktionell ist. Das Gesamtbild entstand durch ein abwechslungsreiches Spiel mit Formen und Baugruppen, die durch starke und kontrastierende Farben gegeneinander abgehoben sind.

› **Ground floor**

› Planta baja

› Erdegeschoss

› **First floor**

› Planta primera

› Erster Stock

› **Second floor**

› Planta segunda

› Zweiter Stock

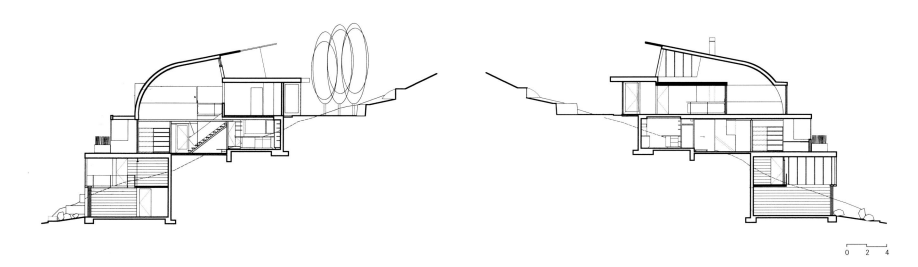

0 2 4

› Sections
› Secciones
› Schnitte

1. What historical reference in particular inspires you when designing a residence?
¿Qué referente histórico en particular le sirve de fuente de inspiración a la hora de proyectar una vivienda?
Welche historische Referenz dient Ihnen als Inspiration beim Entwurf eines Hauses?

2. What is the main factor taken into consideration when designing a residence?
¿Cuál es el principal factor determinante a la hora de diseñar una vivienda?
Welche Rahmenbedingungen, bzw. Faktoren sind für Sie ausschlaggebend beim Konzipieren?

3. What room inside the home do you find most interesting to design?
¿Qué estancia de la vivienda encuentra usted más interesante para diseñar?
Welchen Raum des Hauses finden Sie am spannendsten zu entwerfen?

4. What is your criteria for choosing materials and finishings in a particular room?
¿Cuál es su criterio a la hora de seleccionar los materiales y los acabados en esta estancia?
Welche Kriterien wenden Sie bei der Entscheidung über Materialen und Oberflächen in diesem Raum an?

1. We look at the history of the context, for traces of what came before. We may find and build upon a salient part of that memory, not in a sentimental or representational way, but by an abstraction of or an enactment of it.

2. In our design, the choreography of the human experience precedes the genesis of form.

3. We find interstitial spaces, such as the residual plazas and paseos left from the figure of the buildings to be some of the most interesting places of an urbanscape.

4. We believe in the responsible use of resources, and in the expression of material and structure as an integral part of how the environment is made. Materials can be a kind of chronicle of the building's making; from the concrete foundation walls, the heavy steel structure, the light gauge steel skeleton, the flesh of the plastered walls to infill of the cabinetry and partitions.

1. Tenemos en cuenta la historia del entorno, buscando rastros de lo que hubo antes. Es posible que los encontremos y que la construcción parta de ese recuerdo, no de un modo sentimental o figurativo, sino mediante su abstracción o recreación.

2. En nuestro diseño, la coreografía de la experiencia humana precede a la génesis de la forma.

3. Los espacios, como las plazas y los paseos alejados de los edificios, nos resultan lugares de lo más interesante dentro del paisaje urbano.

4. Creemos en el uso responsable de los recursos y en la expresión del material y la estructura como parte integral de cómo está constituido el entorno. Los materiales pueden ser una especie de crónica de la edificación: desde los cimientos de hormigón, la pesada estructura de metal, el ligero esqueleto de acero hasta las paredes de yeso que albergan el mobiliario y las particiones.

1. Wir beachten stets die Geschichte des Kontexts. Es ist möglich, dass wir Spuren finden und dass der Bau von dieser Erinnerung ausgeht, aber nicht auf sentimentale oder figurative Weise, sondern durch die Abstraktion und Nachahmung der Vergangenheit.

2. In unseren Entwürfen geht der Choreographie der menschlichen Erfahrung die Entstehung der Form voraus.

3. Die Räume wie die Plätze und Gänge, die von den Formen der Gebäude getrennt sind, sind für uns die interessantesten Orte innerhalb der Stadtlandschaft.

4. Für uns ist der verantwortungsvolle Einsatz von Mitteln und die Ausdrucksfähigkeit des Materials und der Struktur als integraler Bestandteil unserer Umgebung von großer Bedeutung. Die Materialien können eine Art Chronik das Baus darstellen, angefangen bei dem Fundament aus Beton, der schweren Metallstruktur, dem leichten Stahlskelett bis hin zu den Gipswänden, in denen Möbel und die Unterteilungen untergebracht sind.

Fung + Blatt Architects, founded in 1990 by Alice Fung and Michael Rosner Blatt, is a firm with five people dedicated to designing residential, commercial, and community projects. Their background in structural design and art results in projects that maintain a balance among structure, architecture, and landscape. This multidisciplinary team believes that the group effort helps all the pieces of a project fit together. They are committed to using resources responsibly in a design that is adapted to the surroundings, that acknowledges the past, and that anticipates the changes in the future of each client.

Fung + Blatt Architects, fundada por Alice Fung y Michael Rosner Blatt en 1990, es una firma compuesta por cinco personas dedicadas al diseño de proyectos residenciales, comerciales y comunitarios. Su formación en diseño de estructuras y arte conduce su trabajo a un permanente análisis entre estructura, arquitectura y paisaje. El grupo cree en la suma de esfuerzos de un equipo pluridisciplinar que contribuye a que encajen todas las piezas de una obra. Está comprometido con el uso responsable de los recursos y en un diseño que se adapta al entorno, comprende el pasado y se anticipa a los cambios del futuro de cada cliente.

Fung + Blatt Architects wurde 1990 von Alice Fung und Michael Rosner Blatt gegründet. Es handelt sich um ein Unternehmen mit 5 Mitarbeitern, die sich dem Entwurf von Wohn-, Geschäfts- und Gemeinschaftsgebäuden widmen. Aufgrund ihrer Ausbildung im Bereich Architektur und Kunst ist die Grundlage ihrer Vorgehensweise eine permanente Analyse der Beziehung zwischen Struktur, Architektur und Landschaft. Sie glauben daran, dass durch die Summierung der Erfahrung und Arbeit eines multidisziplinären Teams ein Ergebnis erreicht wird, bei dem alle Teile in ein Gesamtwerk passen.

☐ This house is located about 250 miles (400 kilometers) from São Paulo, Brazil, on a property with typically exuberant, tropical vegetation. The residence presents two sides that are clearly different yet complementary. From the outside it looks like an austere, contemporary building, but a glance at the exterior patio reveals a type of architecture with references that are clearly traditional. These two languages blend harmoniously, aided by the exterior landscape, which is always present in the home. The outside of the house is faced with mineira stone, which is typical of this region. The cement and natural stone floor, and the wood screens that let in the natural light, provide great warmth to the interior. The single-level home has an L-shape layout, and the peripheral wall on the other two sides defines the patio, which is faced by the bedrooms and the living room.

Du Plessis House

› Marcio Kogan

São Paulo, Brazil › 2003 › Photos © Arnaldo Pappalardo

☐ La casa se encuentra a unos 400 kilómetros de São Paulo, Brasil, en un solar con exuberante vegetación, típicamente tropical. La casa presenta dos aspectos claramente diferenciados y al mismo tiempo complementarios. La apariencia exterior es la de un edificio austero y contemporáneo, mientras que si se echa un vistazo al patio exterior revela una arquitectura con claros referentes tradicionales. Estos dos lenguajes se superponen

☐ Dieses Haus befindet sich 400 Kilometer von São Paulo, Brasilien, entfernt auf einem Grundstück mit einer üppigen, typisch tropischen Vegetation. Das Haus zeigt sich von zwei klar differenzierten Seiten, die sich gegenseitig ergänzen. Von außen handelt es sich um ein nüchternes und zeitgenössisches Haus, während ein Blick durch den Hof eine Architektur zeigt, die offensichtlich von der traditionellen Bauweise beeinflusst ist. Diese bei-

armónicamente apoyándose en el paisaje exterior, presente siempre en la vivienda. El volumen exterior está revestido de piedra mineira, material típico de esta región, y crea una caja que rodea un patio y en el cual se focaliza todo el área social de la casa. El pavimento de cemento y piedra natural así como las celosías de madera, tras las que se filtra la luz natural, otorgan una gran calidez a los interiores. La casa se desarrolla en una sola planta y se presenta un esquema en L, en donde las habitaciones y la sala de estar se abren al patio conformado por el muro perimetral.

den Stile werden harmonisch mit einander kombiniert und durch eine Landschaft ergänzt, die auch im Haus immer präsent ist. Das Gebäude ist von außen mit Natursteinen aus Minas Gerais verkleidet, ein für diese Region typischer Stein, und formt einen Block, der einen Hof umgibt, zu dem hin die Wohn- und Aufenthaltsräume des Hauses liegen. Durch den Boden aus Zement und Naturstein und die Jalousien aus Holz, durch die sich das Tageslicht filtert, wirkt das Innere sehr warm. Das Haus besitzt nur ein Stockwerk und ist in L-Form angelegt. Die Schlafzimmer und das Wohnzimmer liegen zum Hof, der von einer Mauer umgeben wird.

› Ground floor

› Planta baja

› Erdegeschoss

› Side elevation

› Alzado lateral

› Seitenaufriss

› Elevations
› Alzados
› Aufrisse

Marcio Kogan graduated from the Mackenzie School of Architecture in 1976. Since that time he has received many awards for different architectural assignments. He has designed a variety of small-scale and large-scale projects, mainly in Sao Paulo, Brazil and the surrounding area. His architectural work is known for its strong, refined lines. Since 1974 he combines architecture projects with his passion for the cinema. He has created a great number of short films, and his first full-length movie was made in 1988.

Marcio Kogan se graduó en la Escuela de Arquitectura Mackenzie en 1976 y desde entonces ha recibido numerosos premios por varias de sus obras arquitectónicas. Ha diseñado una amplia variedad de proyectos de pequeña y gran escala, principalmente en São Paulo, Brasil, y sus alrededores. Su trabajo como arquitecto, en donde destaca una depurada y contundente línea de diseño, lo combina desde 1974 con su pasión por el cine, disciplina en la que ha realizado numerosos cortometrajes y un primer largo en 1988.

Marcio Kogan schloss sein Studium 1976 an der Mackenzie School of Architecture ab und ist seitdem mit zahlreichen Preisen für verschiedene seiner Bauten ausgezeichnet worden. Er hat eine ganze Reihe kleiner und großer Gebäude hauptsächlich in Sao Paulo, Brasilien, und Umgebung entworfen. Seine Arbeit als Architekt ist vor allem von der Klarheit und Überzeugungskraft seiner Entwürfe gekennzeichnet, die er seit 1974 mit seiner Leidenschaft für das Kino kombiniert. Er hat für eine ganze Reihe von Kurzfilmen und 1988 auch für einen Spielfilm Regie geführt.

☐ This house is located in a residential suburb of Madrid on a generously sized lot. An initial decision was made to place the structure very near the access road to ensure the privacy of the larger part of the property. The general shape was designed like a geode, a natural hole in certain rocks lined with crystals. The building looks like a chunk of granite, solid, dense, and stone-like, contrasting with the large glass openings, which is an analogy of the crystallized part of this artificial geode. There are two levels above ground and a basement; the latter consists of a garage, a sunken patio, and the vertical passageway that leads to the upper levels. The main entrance, on the ground floor, is accessed from the carport. It is protected by an opening in the building that forms a low porch with an overhang. The living, dining, and bathrooms are on this level, which has a spectacular high ceiling. The upper level is used for the bedrooms.

Las Encinas Residence

› Vicens + Ramos

Madrid, Spain › 2003 › Photos © Eugeni Pons

☐ La vivienda se ubica en un barrio residencial de Madrid, en una parcela de generosas proporciones. La primera decisión fue la de ubicar la construcción muy cerca de la vía de acceso y así asegurar la intimidad de la mayor parte de la parcela. El volumen general se concibe como una geoda, un agujero natural en ciertas rocas y tapizado de una sustancia cristalizada. El volumen se presenta como un cuerpo de granito, macizo, cerrado,

☐ Das Haus befindet sich in einem Wohngebiet von Madrid auf einem großen Grundstück. Die erste Entscheidung, die man bei der Planung traf, war es, das Haus in der Nähe der Straße zu errichten und so einen Großteil des Grundstückes als Privatgarten nutzen zu können. Das Gebäude bildet eine Art Geode, eine natürliche Höhlung, die es in manchen Steinen gibt und die von einer kristallisierten Substanz umgeben ist. Das Gebäude

pétreo, que contrasta con las grandes aberturas de vidrio, una analogía de la parte cristalina de esta geoda artificial. La vivienda se desarrolla en dos plantas sobre rasante y una planta sótano, en esta última se ubica el garaje, un patio soterrado y el vestíbulo vertical que conduce a las plantas superiores. El acceso principal, por la planta baja, se produce desde el patio del aparcamiento exterior mediante un retranqueo, a modo de excavación en el volumen y que forma un porche bajo. En esta planta se ubican los espacios de estar, comedor y servicios y cuenta con un espacio de doble altura de gran espectacularidad. La planta superior se dedica a los dormitorios.

hat einen massiven, geschlossenen, steinernen Granitkörper, der einen Gegensatz zu den großen, verglasten Öffnungen bildet, eine Analogie zu dem kristallinen Teil dieser künstlichen Geode. Das Haus hat zwei Stockwerke auf einem Gefälle und ein Kellergeschoss, in dem sich die Garage, ein in den Boden eingelassener Hof und eine vertikale Eingangshalle befinden, die in die oberen Stockwerke führt. Der Haupteingang durch das Erdgeschoss liegt im Hof des Parkplatzes und ist wie eine Ausgrabung am Gebäude, eine Art niedrige Vorhalle angelegt. Im Erdgeschoss liegen das Wohn- und Esszimmer, die Bäder und außerdem ein beeindruckender Raum mit doppelter Höhe. Im Obergeschoss befinden sich die Schlafzimmer.

› Ground floor

› Planta baja

› Erdegeschoss

› First floor

› Planta primera

› Erster Stock

0 3 6

› Elevation
› Alzado
› Aufriss

› Sections
› Secciones
› Schnitte

0 3 6

1. What historical reference in particular inspires you when designing a residence?
   ¿Qué referente histórico en particular le sirve de fuente de inspiración a la hora de proyectar una vivienda?
   Welche historische Referenz dient Ihnen als Inspiration beim Entwurf eines Hauses?

2. What is the main factor taken into consideration when designing a residence?
   ¿Cuál es el principal factor determinante a la hora de diseñar una vivienda?
   Welche Rahmenbedingungen, bzw. Faktoren sind für Sie ausschlaggebend beim Konzipieren?

3. What room inside the home do you find most interesting to design?
   ¿Qué estancia de la vivienda encuentra usted más interesante para diseñar?
   Welchen Raum des Hauses finden Sie am spannendsten zu entwerfen?

4. What is your criteria for choosing materials and finishings in a particular room?
   ¿Cuál es su criterio a la hora de seleccionar los materiales y los acabados en esta estancia?
   Welche Kriterien wenden Sie bei der Entscheidung über Materialen und Oberflächen in diesem Raum an?

1. The architect works from memory. Not just based on history, but drawing selectively and critically from his or her knowledge of history. Therefore, all previous experience is reference material for projects. From this premise, as Quaroni said, history becomes a tool, knowledge of which is indispensable, but once you know it, it cannot be used without interpretation.

2. Architecture is a problem of proportion and balance. There is no single determinant factor but many, whose simultaneous consideration is essential. Good architecture is always complex and satisfies a myriad of functional, design, cultural requirements at the same time.

3. Every room is important and interesting from the standpoint of the house as a whole, as a setting for relationships among the family members, and between them and society.

4. There is no single, previously existing criterium, but criteria that depend on a multitude of factors.

1. El arquitecto proyecta desde la memoria. No sólo a partir de la historia, sino desde la elaboración crítica y selectiva del conocimiento histórico. Así pues, toda la experiencia previa es referencia proyectual.

2. La arquitectura es un problema de proporciones y equilibrios. No hay un factor determinante, sino muchos, cuya consideración simultánea es esencial. La buena arquitectura es siempre compleja y satisface a la vez multitud de requerimientos funcionales, programáticos, culturales, etcétera.

3. Desde la consideración de la vivienda como un conjunto, como un ámbito global de relación familiar y de esta con la sociedad, todas las estancias son igualmente interesantes e importantes.

4. No hay criterio previo, sino criterios que dependen de multitud de factores.

1. Der Architekt entwirft aus dem Gedächtnis. Dabei beruft er sich nicht nur auf die Geschichte, sondern auch auf die kritische und selektive Ausarbeitung seiner historischen Kenntnisse. Deshalb ist jegliche Erfahrung eine Referenz für die Planung.

2. Die Architektur ist ein Problem von Proportionen und Gleichgewichten. Es gibt nicht einen entscheidenden Faktor, sondern viele. Es ist wichtig, sie alle gleichzeitig zu betrachten. Eine gute Architektur ist immer komplex und entspricht gleichzeitig einer Vielzahl von funktionellen, programmatischen, kulturellen, technischen und umweltbedingten Anforderungen....

3. Wenn man eine Wohnung als ein Ganzes betrachtet, als eine globale Umgebung für die familiären Beziehungen und der Beziehungen der Familie zur Gesellschaft, dann sind alle Räume gleich interessant und wichtig.

4. Es gibt kein Kriterium, das schon vorher feststeht, sondern nur Kriterien, die von einer Vielzahl von Faktoren abhängen.

The architecture studio of Vicens + Ramos has been active since 1984. Ignacio Vicens and Hualde is a Professor of Planning in the School of Architecture in Madrid, where he is also the Assistant Director of Doctoral Research and Postgraduate Studies. José Antonio Ramos Abengózar is a Professor of Planning in the same school. The focus of the studio is a combination of professional activity and teaching, which leads to continuous research that feeds the design process. The firm has received numerous awards in Spain for a wide range of projects.

El estudio de arquitectura Vicens + Ramos desarrolla su actividad desde 1984. Ignacio Vicens y Hualde es catedrático de proyectos en la Escuela de Arquitectura de Madrid, en donde al mismo tiempo es subdirector de doctorado, investigación y posgrado. José Antonio Ramos Abengózar es profesor de proyectos en la misma escuela. Compatibilizar la actividad profesional con la enseñanza académica marca la trayectoria del estudio, orientada hacia una continua investigación que alimenta el proceso de diseño. La firma ha recibido numerosos premios en España por varias de sus obra.

Das Architekturbüro Vicens + Ramos besteht seit 1984. Ignacio Vicens y Hualde ist Professor im Bereich Planung an der Architekturschule von Madrid, an der er auch gleichzeitig stellvertretender Direktor für die Dissertationen, Forschung und die postgraduierten Studien ist. José Antonio Ramos Abengózar ist Professor im Bereich Planung an der gleichen Fachhochschule. Diese akademische Lehrtätigkeit prägt auch die Arbeit des Unternehmens, in dem die ständige Forschung die Grundlage für den Gestaltungsprozess bildet. Dem Unternehmen wurden zahlreiche spanische Preise für mehrere Gebäude verschiedener Art verliehen.

☐ The design of this single-family home is based on the fact that today the city of Yokohama is considered one more suburb of the rapidly growing Tokyo metropolitan area. The property, despite being on a hill, has a strong urban feeling, yet it has no tendency towards a specific style. The design approach was based on a review of the conditions of the site and the creation of a series of functions related to each other and to the exterior. The L-shaped configuration allowed the creation of a versatile interior. The different terraces and spaces that face the patio, which resulted from the shape of the house, play off each other to create many scenarios and uses for each room. The extension of the interior spaces towards the outside terraces is emphasized by using the same materials and finishes in both. This approach also created a harmonious relationship between the interior environment and the general context of the neighborhood. From outside, on the other hand, the look proposed for the façade was one of enclosure and austerity to reflect the surrounding structures.

Double-L

› Noriyuki Tajima / tele-design

Yokohama, Japan › 2002 › Photos © Tatsuya Noaki

☐ Debido al increíble crecimiento del área metropolitana de Tokio, la ciudad de Yokohama es actualmente considerada un barrio más de la ciudad. El proyecto para esta vivienda unifamiliar está basado en esta condición. La ubicación del solar, a pesar de encontrarse en una colina, presentaba un marcado carácter urbano sin ningún carácter en particular. La propuesta parte entonces de reconsiderar la condición del lugar y crear una secuencia

☐ Aufgrund des unglaublich schnellen Wachstums des Stadtgebietes von Tokio kann man die Stadt Yokohama heute fast als einen weiteren Vorort von Tokio betrachten. Darauf basiert die Planung für dieses Einfamilienhaus. Es befindet sich auf einem Grundstück, das zwar auf einem Hügel gelegen ist, aber trotzdem einen sehr städtischen und relativ gewöhnlichen Charakter hat. Diese durch das Grundstück vorgegebenen Bedingungen beeinflussten die

de actividades relacionadas entre sí y con el exterior. La forma en L de la composición general permite crear un mundo interior en donde las diferentes terrazas y espacios que miran al patio logrado por esta forma se relacionan entre sí, creando una gran diversidad de situaciones y numerosas maneras de aprovechar cada estancia de la casa. La extensión de los espacios interiores hacia las terrazas exteriores se acentúan con el mismo criterio de acabados y materiales tanto en uno como en otro. Como resultado se logró crear todo un paisaje interior que se relaciona también con el contexto general del barrio. Desde la calle se propuso una fachada cerrada y austera que dialoga con el entorno construido.

Planung in der Weise, dass man versuchte, eine Reihe von miteinander und mit der Außenwelt verbundenen Elementen zu schaffen. Durch die Anlage einer L-Form entstand eine innere Welt, in der verschiedene Terrassen und Räume, die zum Hof liegen, miteinander in Beziehung stehen, so dass viele verschiedene Situationen und räumliche Möglichkeiten in dem Haus entstehen. Die Tatsache, dass die Innenräume auf die Außenterrassen hin ausgerichtet sind, wird noch durch die verwendeten Materialien in den Räumen und auf den Terrassen unterstrichen. So entstand eine innere Landschaft, die auch mit dem allgemeinen Kontext des Viertels in Verbindung steht. Von der Straße aus wirkt die Fassade geschlossen und nüchtern, jedoch gut in die bebaute Umgebung integriert.

0   2   4

› **Ground floor**

› Planta baja

› Erdegeschoss

› **First floor**

› Planta primera

› Erster Stock

› **Sections**

› Secciones

› Schnitte

› Elevations
› Alzados
› Aufrisse

› Diagrams
› Esquemas
› Schema

1. What historical reference in particular inspires you when designing a residence?

   ¿Qué referente histórico en particular le sirve de fuente de inspiración a la hora de proyectar una vivienda?

   Welche historische Referenz dient Ihnen als Inspiration beim Entwurf eines Hauses?

2. What is the main factor taken into consideration when designing a residence?

   ¿Cuál es el principal factor determinante a la hora de diseñar una vivienda?

   Welche Rahmenbedingungen, bzw. Faktoren sind für Sie ausschlaggebend beim Konzipieren?

3. What room inside the home do you find most interesting to design?

   ¿Qué estancia de la vivienda encuentra usted más interesante para diseñar?

   Welchen Raum des Hauses finden Sie am spannendsten zu entwerfen?

4. What is your criteria for choosing materials and finishings in a particular room?

   ¿Cuál es su criterio a la hora de seleccionar los materiales y los acabados en esta estancia?

   Welche Kriterien wenden Sie bei der Entscheidung über Materialen und Oberflächen in diesem Raum an?

---

1. I don't have particular example but have some influences from historical Japanese residences and also 30's to 70's modern houses. Recently my interest moves to more 70's houses.

2. Three things in combination: Activities of the dwellers, natural environment such as light, wind and landscape, and urban context.

3. I am interested in more of erasing the separation of rooms and functions, trying to find flow of activities and living condition by connecting them, a house becomes more one room connected.

4. I do not choose materials which have too much strong expression, but I do rather use materials suitable to spatial compositions. Occasionally I use stronger material in order to emphasize its spatial quality. Mostly uses neutral material such as white walls.

---

1. No puedo nombrar a nadie en particular, pero sí tengo influencias de residencias japonesas históricas y también de casa modernas construidas entre los años 1930 y 1970. En la actualidad, mis intereses se mueven más cerca de las casa de la década de los setenta.

2. Tres factores combinados: las actividades de los residentes, el entorno natural (la luz, el viento, el paisaje) y el contexto urbano.

3. Estoy interesado en eliminar las separaciones de espacios y funciones y encontrar un flujo de actividades y condiciones de vida con la conexión de las estancias, de modo que la casa se convierte en una gran habitación interconectada.

4. No elijo materiales que tengan una expresión demasiado marcada, sino materiales que permitan crear combinaciones espaciales. Ocasionalmente uso materiales más fuertes con el fin de acentuar las cualidades del espacio. En la mayoría de los casos utilizo materiales neutros, como las paredes blancas.

---

1. Ich kann niemanden im Besonderen erwähnen, aber ich bin beeinflusst von den historischen japanischen Häusern, und auch von den modernen Häusern, die zwischen den Dreißiger- und Siebzigerjahren gebaut wurden. Im Augenblick interessiere ich mich mehr für die Häuser der Siebzigerjahre

2. Drei kombinierte Faktoren, die Aktivitäten der Bewohner, die natürliche Umgebung (Licht, Wind, Landschaft) und der städtische Kontext.

3. Ich versuche, die Trennung zwischen Räumen und Funktionen aufzuheben, und so ein Fließen der Aktivitäten und Lebensbedingungen zu erreichen, indem ich die Räume miteinander verbinde. So wird aus dem Haus ein großer, verbundener Raum.

4. Ich entscheide mich nicht für Materialien, die einen zu starken Ausdruck haben, sondern für Materialien, die sich auf besondere Art kombinieren lassen. Manchmal benutze ich starke Materialien, um eine Eigentümlichkeit des Raumes zu unterstreichen. Meist setze ich neutrale Materialien wie weiße Wände ein.

Tele-design was established with the purpose of incorporating two important tendencies of contemporary Japanese society into the vision and structure of the company. The first was the pursuit of new models of economic growth, and the second was the rapid development of telecommunications within the global economy. In this way design becomes a tool for exploration as well as a vehicle for the incorporation of the latest technologies. Tele-design consists of a multi-disciplinary team that has worked together since 1999. Its unique structure has caught the attention of clients, the press and international critics.

Tele-design se estableció con ánimo de incorporar dos tendencias significativas de la actual sociedad japonesa en la visión y estructura de la compañía. En primer lugar, la búsqueda de nuevos modelos tras el crecimiento económico y en segundo lugar, el rápido desarrollo de las telecomunicaciones en la economía global. De esta manera, el diseño se convierte en una herramienta para explorar y nutrirse de las últimas tecnologías. Por este motivo, tele-design está formado por un equipo pluridisciplinar que colabora junto desde 1999. Su particular estructura ha llamado la atención no sólo de clientes, sino de la prensa y la crítica internacional.

Tele-design wurde gegründet, um zwei wichtige Tendenzen der heutigen japanischen Gesellschaft in die Unternehmensstruktur zu integrieren. Diese Tendenzen sind die Suche nach neuen Modellen nach dem starken Wirtschaftswachstum und die schnelle Entwicklung der Telekommunikationen in der globalen Wirtschaft. So wurde das Design zu einem Werkzeug, um die neusten Technologien zu erforschen und sich von ihnen zu nähren. Tele-design arbeitet daher seit 1999 mit ein em multidisziplinäres Team. Diese besondere Struktur erweckte viel Aufmerksamkeit seitens der Kunden und der internationalen Presse und Kritik.

ATTICS

ÁTICOS / DACHWOHMENG

☐ One of the main interests of this architect, which is seen in all his projects, is the manipulation of light as a design element. His interest is not only in illuminating spaces, but also in using the light as a medium for imprinting a specific character on each area of the project. In this case the approach is complemented by the personalities of the clients, two movie producers who are seduced by bright and strong colors. The design had to resolve two residential scenarios that could function independently within the same long and narrow, two-level unit. To make up for the lack of light in this layout, typical of New York, the architect took advantage of the fact that the unit was on the top floor of the building to create a skylight that illuminates all the central part of the residence. The existing walls on the top floor, where the living and eating areas are located, were removed to create an open space that enhances the feeling of space and light.

Phillipps / Skaife Residence

› Alden Maddry Architect

New York, NY, USA › 2002 › Photos © Jordi Miralles

☐ Una de las principales inquietudes en la trayectoria profesional de este arquitecto es la utilización de la luz como herramienta de diseño. Su interés radica no sólo en iluminar los espacios, sino en aprovechar la iluminación como medio para imprimir un rasgo específico a cada ámbito del proyecto. En el caso de este proyecto, se complementa con el carácter de sus clientes, una pareja de productores cinematográficos, a quienes les seduce los

☐ Dieser Architekt hat sich während seiner ganzen Laufbahn intensiv mit dem Licht als Gestaltungselement auseinandergesetzt. Dabei geht es nicht einfach nur darum, die Räume zu beleuchten, sondern die Beleuchtung als ein Mittel zu benutzen, um jedem Bereich eines Gebäudes einen besonderen Charakter zu verleihen. Im Falle dieses Bauwerkes wird diese Vorbedingung noch durch den Charakter der Kunden ergänzt. Es han-

colores intensos y brillantes. El diseño debía resolver dos programas de vivienda que funcionaran independientemente dentro de una misma unidad compuesta de dos plantas prolongadas. Para contrarrestar la falta de luz que generalmente hay en este tipo de configuración típica en Nueva York, se aprovechó que el volumen está situado en la última planta del edificio para crear una claraboya central que iluminara toda la parte central de la vivienda. La planta superior, en donde se ubican las zonas de estar y comedor, se liberaron de paredes existentes y se logró un espacio abierto en el que se acentúa aún más la sensación de amplitud y luminosidad.

delt sich um ein Paar, das Kinofilme produziert und sich gerne von starken und glänzenden Farben verführen lässt. Durch die Gestaltung sollten zwei unabhängige Wohnbereiche innerhalb einer Einheit von zwei langen und engen Stockwerken untergebracht werden. Um den Lichtmangel auszugleichen, der normalerweise bei einer solchen, für New York typischen Gebäudeform herrscht, wurde die Tatsache ausgenutzt, dass die Räume sich im obersten Stockwerk des Gebäudes befinden und es wurde ein zentrales Dachfenster eingebaut, durch das Licht für den gesamten, mittleren Teil der Wohnung fällt. Im oberen Stockwerk, wo sich die Wohn- und Speisezimmer befinden, beseitigte man alle Wände, um einen offenen, weit und hell wirkenden Raum zu schaffen.

0   1   2

› Ground floor

› Planta baja

› Erdegeschoss

› First floor

› Planta primera

› Erster Stock

› Axonometry

› Axonometría

› Axonometrie

1. What historical reference in particular inspires you when designing a residence?
   ¿Qué referente histórico en particular le sirve de fuente de inspiración a la hora de proyectar una vivienda?
   Welche historische Referenz dient Ihnen als Inspiration beim Entwurf eines Hauses?

2. What is the main factor taken into consideration when designing a residence?
   ¿Cuál es el principal factor determinante a la hora de diseñar una vivienda?
   Welche Rahmenbedingungen, bzw. Faktoren sind für Sie ausschlaggebend beim Konzipieren?

3. What room inside the home do you find most interesting to design?
   ¿Qué estancia de la vivienda encuentra usted más interesante para diseñar?
   Welchen Raum des Hauses finden Sie am spannendsten zu entwerfen?

4. What is your criteria for choosing materials and finishings in a particular room?
   ¿Cuál es su criterio a la hora de seleccionar los materiales y los acabados en esta estancia?
   Welche Kriterien wenden Sie bei der Entscheidung über Materialen und Oberflächen in diesem Raum an?

---

1. I draw inspiration from masterful individual houses and living spaces that range from the Maison de Verre in Paris to the Katsura Imperial Villa in Kyoto. But I have also drawn many ideas for my work from relatively unknown unpublished vernacular work from across the world.

2. How can I create spaces that will inspire my clients and enhance their experience of living.

3. There is not one particular room type that I find is consistently the most interesting to design. In fact the design of the interstitial spaces and connections between rooms can often be more interesting and add more to the design of the home than the composition of the individual rooms.

4. First I determine what function(s) the surface I am choosing will have. And by "function" I am not just talking about utilitarian concerns. Given these criteria I search for a possible material that can meet these requirements.

---

1. Encuentro inspiración en varios ejemplos famosos de proyectos de vivienda, desde la Maison de Verre en París hasta la Villa Imperial Katsura en Kioto. Pero también he aplicado muchas ideas en mi trabajo tomadas de obras vernaculares, desconocidas y poco publicadas alrededor del mundo.

2. Cómo puedo crear espacios que servirán de inspiración a mis clientes y realzar su experiencia de habitabilidad.

3. No hay una tipo de habitación en concreto que encuentre más interesante para diseñar. De hecho, el diseño de los espacios intersticiales y las conexiones entre habitaciones pueden ser más interesantes y aportar más al diseño de la casa que la composición de habitaciones individuales.

4. Primero determino qué función, y no solamente en términos utilitarios, tendrá la superficie que estoy eligiendo y con este criterio definido busco posibles materiales que puedan sustituir estas necesidades.

---

1. Mich inspirieren verschiedene Beispiele berühmter Planungen für Wohnhäuser, angefangen bei dem Maison de Verre in Paris bis zur Kaiserstadt Katsura in Kyoto. Ich habe aber auch viele Ideen in meinen Arbeiten umgesetzt, die aus volkstümlichen, architektonischen Werken stammen, und die weltweit relativ unbekannt sind und selten veröffentlicht wurden.

2. Wie kann ich Räume schaffen, die meine Kunden inspirieren und ihre Erfahrung im Wohnen betonen.

3. Es gibt keinen besonderen Typ Raum, den ich interessanter als andere finde. Tatsächlich kann die Gestaltung von Zwischenräumen und Verbindungen zwischen den verschiedenen Zimmern interessanter sein und mehr zum Design eines Hauses beitragen als die Gestaltung der individuellen Räume.

4. Zunächst bestimme ich die Funktion, nicht nur im Bezug auf die Benutzung, und sie wird die Fläche einnehmen, die ich wähle. Nachdem dieses Kriterium definiert wurde, wähle ich die möglichen Materialien für diese Bestimmung.

Alden Maddry Architect was founded in the spring of 1996. The firm specializes in cultural and residential designs, and projects related to art, in New York City and the surrounding area. Maddry is especially interested in the construction details and depends on the talent of expert workers and artisans of the region to carry out their projects. They have used alternative energy sources, — solar and geothermal — in many of their past projects.

Alden Maddry Architect fue fundada en primavera de 1996. La firma está especializada en diseños culturales y residenciales y en proyectos relacionados con el arte desarrollados en la ciudad de Nueva York y sus alrededores. Maddry está especialmente interesado en los procesos de construcción y se apoya en el talento de trabajadores y en artesanos expertos de la región para conformar sus proyectos. Fuentes de energía alternativa, como la energía solar o la geotermal, han sido utilizadas en proyectos pasados.

Alden Maddry Architect wurde im Frühjahr 1996 gegründet. Das Unternehmen ist auf Projekte in den Bereichen Kunst, Kultur und Stadtwohnungen in New York und Umgebung spezialisiert. Bei Maddry interessiert man sich besonders für die Bauprozesse; und die Arbeiten werden in Zusammenarbeit mit begabten Arbeitern und Handwerkern aus der Region durchgeführt. In vielen, bereits von Maddry errichteten Gebäuden wurde alternative Energiequellen wie Solarenergie oder Erdwärme benutzt.

☐ The Abbot Kinney neighborhood in Venice, California, is rapidly becoming an artist's district. A growing number of designers, multimedia firms, and artists choose this neighborhood, which is turning into a lively and diverse community. These professionals are not only looking for a section of the city that identifies with their way of life, but also for interior spaces that adapt to their requirements. They are searching for more casual, informal, and flexible environments that allow them to live and work in the same space. This project consists of a typical adaptation of the traditional artist's loft, with large, open spaces that can be used for living or working, as required. The plan includes three different adjacent lofts that share the same structure, materials, and color palette, giving it the appearance of a compact building. These characteristics allow the creation of a continuous façade and a commercial row facing the street. All the units are separated by patios and are equipped with balconies, terraces, and glassed-in areas.

Abbot Kinney Lofts

› Mark Mack Architects

Venice, CA, USA › 2001 › Photos © Undine Pröhl

☐ El barrio de Abbot Kinney, en Venice, California, se está convirtiendo rápidamente en un distrito de artistas. Cada año crece el número de diseñadores, firmas multimedias y artistas que escogen este sector para emplazar sus estudios y crear una comunidad diversa y vital. Esta nueva cultura de profesionales no sólo busca un sector de la ciudad que se identifique con su modo de vida, sino también espacios interiores que se adapten a sus necesi-

☐ Abbot Kinney in Venice, Kalifornien, entwickelt sich zur Zeit zunehmend zu einem Künstlerviertel. Jedes Jahr gibt es mehr Designer, Multimedia-Unternehmen und Künstler, die sich dieses Viertel für ihre Studios aussuchen, wodurch eine vielseitige und lebendige Gemeinschaft entstanden ist. Diese Menschen in kreativen Berufen suchen nicht nur ein Viertel in der Stadt, das ihrem Lebensstil zusagt, sondern auch Räume, die ihren

dades. Entornos más casuales, informales, flexibles, que permitan vivir y trabajar en una misma superficie, son las principales características de esta búsqueda. Este proyecto consiste en una adaptación tipológica del tradicional loft de artistas en el que se crea espacios amplios y abiertos que permiten ser usados como vivienda o zona de trabajo según las necesidades. El conjunto está compuesto por tres diferentes lofts adyacentes que comparten misma estructura, materiales y paleta de colores, de esta manera toma la apariencia de una unidad. Esto contribuye a crear una fachada continua y un paseo comercial orientado a la calle, mientras que cada uno de los volúmenes está separado por patios y disfruta de zonas acristaladas, balcones y terrazas.

Bedürfnissen entsprechen. Weniger strenge, flexible und moderne Räume, in denen man gleichzeitig leben und arbeiten kann, werden besonders gesucht. Dieses Projekt besteht in einer typischen Gestaltung eines traditionellen Künstler-Loftes, in dem weite und offene Räume geschaffen werden, die man sowohl zum Wohnen als auch zum Arbeiten benutzen kann. Das Gebäude beherbergt drei benachbarte Lofts, die die gleiche Struktur, Materialien und Farbpalette teilen, so dass ein zusammenhängendes Ganzes entsteht. So konnte auch eine durchgehende Fassade und ein kommerziell genutzter Weg zur Straße hin geschaffen werden, während alle Lofts durch Höfe getrennt sind und ihre eigenen verglasten Bereiche, Balkone und Terrassen haben.

› Ground floor

› Planta baja

› Erdegeschoss

› First floor

› Planta primera

› Erster Stock

› Second floor

› Planta segunda

› Zweiter Stock

› Elevations
› Alzados
› Aufrisse

› Sections
› Secciones
› Schnitte

Mark Mack, along with his former partner Andrew Batey, earned his reputation as an architect in California mainly for his single-family home and villa designs in the early 1980's. He established his own office in San Francisco in 1984 and then moved to Venice, California in 1993. His approach to design is influenced by his academic work and restless curiosity. He was a professor in the School of Architecture at the University of California, Los Angeles. He was also a cofounder of Archetype Magazine and has contributed numerous articles to different magazines.

Mark Mack, junto a su antiguo socio Andrew Batey, se ha ganado su reputación como arquitecto en California principalmente por el diseño de villas y casas unifamiliares al inicio de la década de 1980. Estableció su propia oficina en San Francisco en 1984 y posteriormente se desplazó a Venice, California, en 1993. Su acercamiento al diseño está influenciado por sus inquietudes y su trabajo académico. Fue profesor de la Escuela de Arquitectura en la Universidad de California, Los Ángeles; asimismo fue cofundador de la revista Archetype Magazine y colaborador en numerosos artículos en diversas publicaciones.

Mark Mack begann seine Karriere Anfang der Achtzigerjahre mit der Planung von Einfamilienhäusern und Villen in Kalifornien zusammen mit seinem ehemaligen Teilhaber Andrew Batey. 1984 gründete er in San Francisco sein eigenes Unternehmen, das er 1993 nach Venice, Kalifornien, verlegte. Seine Interessen und seine akademische Arbeit beeinflussen stark seinen Gestaltungsstil. Er war Professor am Fachbereich Architektur der Universität von Kalifornien in Los Angeles. Ebenso war er Mitbegründer der Zeitschrift Archetype Magazine, in der er zahlreiche Artikel veröffentlicht hat.

☐ This project is located in a space that was originally occupied by a lighting factory in an industrial neighborhood of the borough of Brooklyn, New York. The project had to fulfill the expectations of the clients, two artists from Brazil who wanted a loft-style space that would provide various settings for living as well as for working. A translucent, retractable wall defines the different areas in the lower level and adds character to the space. The natural light from a skylight flows through the translucent wall to illuminate the interior of the loft's living area. A dramatic metal stairway, light and equally transparent, connects the lower level with the top level where the bedrooms and an outdoor terrace are found. At the same time the stairway serves as an esthetic reference to the industrial nature of the building's past. The original façade, consisting of a garage door, and the new aluminum and wood features emphasize the contrast between the warm and organic interior and the heavy and metallic materials of the exterior.

Brooklyn Loft

› Basil Walter Architects

New York, NY, USA › 2002 › Photos © Bilyana Dimitrova

☐ El proyecto se ubica en un terreno que fue originalmente ocupado por una fábrica de iluminación en el
barrio industrial del distrito de Brooklyn, en Nueva York. El
proyecto debía cumplir las expectativas de los clientes,
una pareja brasileña de artistas, que querían disponer de
un espacio tipo loft que evocara situaciones diversas
tanto para vivir como para trabajar. Una pared retráctil y
translúcida define y otorga carácter a las diferentes zonas

☐ Dieses Gebäude befindet sich auf einem Grundstück
im Industrieviertel von Brooklyn, New York, auf dem einst
eine Lampenfabrik stand. Die Kunden, ein brasilianisches
Künstlerpaar, wünschten sich eine Art Loft, in dem man
sowohl wohnen als auch arbeiten kann. Eine einziehbare
und lichtdurchlässige Wand definiert und bereichert die
verschiedenen Zonen im Erdgeschoss. Das Tageslicht
dringt über ein Dachfenster ein und filtert sich durch die

en la planta baja del espacio. La luz natural que descien-
de de la claraboya se filtra por la pared translúcida e ilu-
mina el interior de la zona de la vivienda. Una dramática
escalera metálica, ligera y transparente, conecta la planta baja con el nivel superior en donde se ubican las habitaciones y una terraza exterior. La escalera, por otra
parte, sirve como recuerdo estético de la antigua naturaleza industrial del edificio en el pasado. La fachada original, compuesta por una puerta de garaje, y la
nueva terraza de aluminio y madera acentúan el contraste entre el cálido interior orgánico y los detalles metálicos
y pesados del exterior.

lichtdurchlässige Wand, so dass auch das Innere des
Wohnbereiches beleuchtet wird. Eine dramatisch wirkende, leichte und ebenfalls transparente Metalltreppe verbindet das Erdgeschoss mit dem Obergeschoss, in dem
sich die Schlafzimmer und die Terrasse im Freien befinden. Die Treppe dient auch als ästhetische Anspielung
auf die industrielle Vergangenheit des Gebäudes. Die
Originalfassade, die aus einer Garagentür besteht, und
die neue Terrasse aus Aluminium und Holz unterstreichen
den deutlich erkennbaren Unterschied zwischen den
warm und organisch wirkenden Materialien im Inneren
und den schweren Details aus Metall außen.

› **Ground floor**

› Planta baja

› Erdegeschoss

› **First floor**

› Planta primera

› Erster Stock

0   2   4

1. What historical reference in particular inspires you when designing a residence?
¿Qué referente histórico en particular le sirve de fuente de inspiración a la hora de proyectar una vivienda?
Welche historische Referenz dient Ihnen als Inspiration beim Entwurf eines Hauses?

2. What is the main factor taken into consideration when designing a residence?
¿Cuál es el principal factor determinante a la hora de diseñar una vivienda?
Welche Rahmenbedingungen, bzw. Faktoren sind für Sie ausschlaggebend beim Konzipieren?

3. What room inside the home do you find most interesting to design?
¿Qué estancia de la vivienda encuentra usted más interesante para diseñar?
Welchen Raum des Hauses finden Sie am spannendsten zu entwerfen?

4. What is your criteria for choosing materials and finishings in a particular room?
¿Cuál es su criterio a la hora de seleccionar los materiales y los acabados en esta estancia?
Welche Kriterien wenden Sie bei der Entscheidung über Materialen und Oberflächen in diesem Raum an?

1. It is the reference to historical methods rather than any direct period references which find their way most consistently into our work. A study of historical systems of design and construction creates a process that integrates time tested methods with free-thinking inventiveness.

2. What is most important is keeping the brightest torch shining firmly on those qualities of the house that make it beautiful, functional and economical and not getting sidetracked during the process. This requires continual reserves of energy and patience.

3. It is the connections between the various rooms or spaces in a home that pose the most challenging design issues.

4. The space itself must be the dominant image. Instances of local color or pattern must complement the effect of the space itself, and not the other way around.

1. En nuestro trabajo utilizamos habitualmente referencias a métodos históricos más que a periodos concretos. Un estudio de sistemas históricos de diseño y construcción constituye un proceso que integra métodos probados en una inventiva escéptica.

2. Lo más importante es realzar las cualidades que hacen que una vivienda sea bella, funcional y económica, sin que caigan en el olvido durante el proceso. Esto requiere continuas reservas de energía y paciencia.

3. Los elementos que presentan el mayor desafío durante el proceso de diseño son las conexiones entre las diferentes habitaciones o áreas.

4. El espacio en sí mismo debe ser la imagen dominante. Los elementos puntuales de color o forma deben complementar el efecto del espacio, no al revés.

1. Bei unserer Arbeit benutzen wir normalerweise eher Referenzen auf historische Methoden als auf konkrete Epochen der Zeitgeschichte. Eine Studie der historischen Systeme bei der Gestaltung und beim Bau stellt einen Prozess dar, der erprobte Methoden in eine skeptische Erfindungsgabe integriert.

2. Es ist wichtig, die Eigenschaften zu betonen, die dafür sorgen, dass ein Haus oder eine Wohnung schön, funktionell und ökonomisch werden. Diese Eigenschaften darf man während des Gesamtprozesses nicht vergessen, und dazu braucht man ständige Energie und Geduldsreserven.

3. Die Elemente, die die größte Herausforderung beim Planungsprozess darstellen, sind die Verbindungen zwischen den verschiedenen Räumen und Bereichen.

4. Der Raum selbst sollte das dominierende Bild sein. Einzelne, farbige Elemente oder Formen sollten die Wirkung des Raumes ergänzen, und nicht umgekehrt.

Basil Walter Architects was officially launched in 2001 after practicing for twelve years as Sweeny Walter Architects, founded in 1998. Today it is an organization of 13 architects and designers led by Basil Walter and his associate Brenda Bello. Basil Walter Architects and his previous firm were responsible for a variety of projects ranging from private residences to design offices and event planning. The firm, based in New York City, has ample experience in designing emblematic buildings as well as in renovating the interiors of many apartments in historic buildings.

Basil Walter Architects comenzó oficialmente en el año 2001 después de 12 años de trabajo como Sweeny Walter Architects, fundada en 1998. En la actualidad, es una organización de 13 arquitectos y diseñadores liderados por Basil Walter y su socia Brenda Bello. Basil Walter Architects y su firma predecesora han sido responsables del diseño de una amplia variedad de proyectos que se extienden desde viviendas privadas hasta oficinas de diseño o montaje de eventos. La firma, con sede en Nueva York, tiene amplia experiencia en el diseño de edificios emblemáticos así como en la reforma de apartamentos en edificios históricos.

Basil Walter Architects wurde offiziell 2001 gegründet, nachdem bereits 12 Jahre unter dem Namen Sweeny Walter Architects, gegründet 1989, gearbeitet wurde. Heute arbeiten 13 freie Architekten und Innenarchitekten für Basil Walter und seine Gesellschafterin Brenda Bello. Basil Walter Architects und die Vorgängerfirma haben bereits sehr verschiedene Planungen durchgeführt, Privatwohnungen, edle Büroräume und Bauten für Veranstaltungen. In New York blickt man auf eine lange Erfahrung in der Planung von emblematischen Gebäuden und Innenrenovierung von Wohnungen in historischen Gebäuden zurück.

This project is located in an old industrial space in the 11th District in Paris. It is not a typical industrial building with a horizontal, open, and fluid space, but one that is vertical and sturdy, made of wood and metal covered with rustic walls of exposed brick. The interior was opened up by removing all the dividing walls to create a naturally illuminated space of generous proportions. The structural and architectural elements that define and create the character of the interior space were preserved. The vertical aspect of the building offered the opportunity to create a design that exceeded the limits of a traditional loft. The project attempted to create a vertical sequence that highlight the dynamism of the design. Making an analogy to a movie script, the design lays out a sequence between what is seen, what is not seen, and what one hopes to see, all integrated into a common setting. The building was left completely intact, and certain aspects of the design took the form of solid spaces with opaque and translucent qualities. These volumes become anecdotes within the sequence.

Vertical Loft

› Insite Architecture Design

Paris, France › 2003 › Photos © Georges Fessy

☐ El proyecto se ubica en un antiguo terreno industrial en el distrito 11 de París. No se trata de la típica nave industrial en donde se plantearía un esquema en horizontal, abierto y fluido, sino que consiste en una estructura robusta de madera y metal que presenta una composición en vertical envuelta por una pared de aspecto rústico de ladrillo a la vista. Se liberó el espacio interior, eliminando todas las divisiones interiores, para obtener un

☐ Dieses Loft befindet sich in einem ehemaligen Industriegebäude im 11. Arrondissement von Paris. Es handelt sich nicht um das typische Fabrikgebäude mit einem horizontalen, offenen und fließenden Aufbau, sondern um eine robuste Struktur aus Holz und Metall, die sich vertikal aufbaut und von einer rustikalen Wand aus unverputztem Ziegelstein umgeben ist. Die Innenräume wurden erweitert, indem man alle Zwischenwände abriss.

espacio diáfano y de generosas proporciones. Se mantuvieron y rescataron los elementos estructurales y arquitectónicos que definen y subrayan el carácter del espacio interior. La naturaleza vertical del volumen ofrecía una oportunidad para crear un proyecto que fuera más allá de los límites del loft tradicional. El proyecto debía crear una secuencia en vertical que revelara el dinamismo del programa. A semejanza de un guión cinematográfico, el diseño plantea una secuencia entre lo que se ve, lo que no se ve y lo que se espera ver relacionado por un escenario común. El volumen se respetó en su totalidad y ciertos aspectos del programa se materializaron en forma de piezas sólidas de cualidades translúcidas u opacas. Estos volúmenes se convierten en anécdotas dentro de la secuencia.

So erreichte man großzügige Proportionen und ließ das Tageslicht in die Räume eindringen. Die strukturellen und architektonischen Elemente, die die Räume prägen, wurden beibehalten und wieder hergestellt. Die vertikale Gliederung des Gebäudes machte es möglich, Räumlichkeiten zu schaffen, in denen mehr Kreativität als in einer traditionellen Fabriketage möglich war. Es wurde eine vertikale Sequenz geschaffen, die die Dynamik der Planung zeigte. Analog zu dem Drehbuch eines Films wird mit der Gestaltung eine Sequenz vorgeschlagen, eine Sequenz zwischen dem, was man sieht, dem was man nicht sieht und dem, was man zu sehen erwartet, all das am gleichen Schauplatz. Die Formen wurden absolut respektiert und bestimmte Aspekte der Gestaltung zeigten sich in festen Elementen, die doch lichtdurchlässig oder opak sind. Diese Formen werden zu Anekdoten innerhalb einer Sequenz.

0   2   4

› Ground floor

› Planta baja

› Erdegeschoss

› First floor

› Planta primera

› Erster Stock

› Second floor

› Planta segunda

› Zweiter Stock

0 1 2

> Longitudinal section

› Sección longitudinal

› Längaufreiss

> Transversal section

› Sección transversal

› Querschnitt

1. What historical reference in particular inspires you when designing a residence?
¿Qué referente histórico en particular le sirve de fuente de inspiración a la hora de proyectar una vivienda?
Welche historische Referenz dient Ihnen als Inspiration beim Entwurf eines Hauses?

2. What is the main factor taken into consideration when designing a residence?
¿Cuál es el principal factor determinante a la hora de diseñar una vivienda?
Welche Rahmenbedingungen, bzw. Faktoren sind für Sie ausschlaggebend beim Konzipieren?

3. What room inside the home do you find most interesting to design?
¿Qué estancia de la vivienda encuentra usted más interesante para diseñar?
Welchen Raum des Hauses finden Sie am spannendsten zu entwerfen?

4. What is your criteria for choosing materials and finishings in a particular room?
¿Cuál es su criterio a la hora de seleccionar los materiales y los acabados en esta estancia?
Welche Kriterien wenden Sie bei der Entscheidung über Materialen und Oberflächen in diesem Raum an?

1. We look at the social and built history of the region. We dissect these events and the periods that seem most pertinent to the project at hand and us.

2. There are several factors that cannot be left to the side. The history of the site, the program, which is most often stipulated by the client, and probably the most important factor is the intrinsic value-system of the client and how this system matches your own.

3. All. A house is not comprised of a series of discreet design instances, but rather is a puzzle of its different parts, so one 'room' cannot be more interesting than the other.

4. The site and the type of project dictate the materials. Then there are of course the individual economics of a project that play an important role when the final decision making takes place.

1. Nos fijamos en la historia social y arquitectónica de la región. Diseccionamos estos acontecimientos y los periodos que nos parecen más adecuados para el proyecto y para nosotros.

2. Hay varios factores que no pueden dejarse de lado. La historia del lugar, el programa, el cual está casi siempre estipulado por el cliente; y probablemente el factor más importante sea la escala de valores del cliente y cómo esta se corresponde con la nuestra.

3. Todas. Una casa no está formada por una serie de diseños individuales, sino por un puzzle que une sus diferentes partes, así que una habitación no puede ser más importante que otra.

4. El solar y el tipo de proyecto dictan los materiales que utilizamos. También hay que tener en cuenta el presupuesto, ya que es muy importante a la hora de tomar decisiones.

1. Wir sehen uns die soziale und architektonische Geschichte der Region genau an und versuchen, die Ereignisse in Erfahrung zu bringen, die einen Teil dieser Geschichte bilden. Wir analysieren diese Ereignisse und Zeiträume, die uns für unsere Planung und uns selbst am angemessensten erscheinen.

2. Es gibt mehrere Faktoren, die man unbedingt berücksichtigen muss. Die Geschichte des Ortes, die notwendigen Wohnfunktionen, die fast immer vom Kunden festgelegt werden. Der wahrscheinlich wichtigste Faktor ist die Werteskala des Kunden und wie diese mit der unseren übereinstimmt.

3. Alle. Ein Haus besteht nicht aus einer Reihe von individuellen Entwürfen, sondern aus einem Puzzle, das seine verschiedenen Teile zusammenfügt. Deshalb kann ein Raum nicht wichtiger als ein anderer sein.

4. Das Grundstück und die Art des Bauvorhabens geben uns die Materialien vor, die wir benutzen. Man muss auch das Budget berücksichtigen, da es die Entscheidungen wesentlich beeinflusst.

Insite Architecture Design is a multi-disciplinary firm that groups architects, designers, and consultants into teams that encompass architecture, the environment, and design. The diverse talents include specialties in urban planning, architecture, landscape architecture, design, communication, and graphic design that work together to develop new environments and creative processes within the context of a global media and technology. They are considered neither modern nor neo-modern. Their approach is based on an optimistic vision of architecture, technology, and global culture.

Insite Architecture Design es una firma multidisciplinar que agrupa arquitectos, diseñadores y consultores en un equipo que aborda las áreas de arquitectura, medio ambiente y diseño. Los diversos talentos que componen el grupo, especializados en urbanismo, arquitectura, paisajismo, diseño, comunicación y diseño gráfico, trabajan juntos para desarrollar nuevos entornos y procesos de creación dentro de un contexto de globalización de medios y tecnología. No se consideran modernos, ni neomodernos. Su creencia parte de una visión optimista de la arquitectura, la tecnología y la cultura global.

Insite Architecture Design ist ein multidisziplinäres Unternehmen, in dem Architekten, Innenarchitekten und Berater innerhalb eines Netzes tätig sind, das sich mit den Bereichen Architektur, Umwelt und Design befasst. Die verschiedenen Mitarbeiter der Gruppe sind Spezialisten in Städtebau, Architektur, Landschaftsplanung, Innenarchitektur, Kommunikation und Grafik und arbeiten zusammen, um neue Umgebungen und Gestaltungsprozesse innerhalb eines Kontextes der Globalisierung der Mittel und Technologie zu schaffen. Sie halten an einer optimistischen Vision der Architektur, Technologie und der globalen Kultur fest.

☐ The architect treated this house as if it were the framework of a car, in which the concept of luxury is signified by the austerity of its interior rather than by the excessive use of objects. The main exercise in this project consisted of paring down rather than adding. The simplicity of the space is enhanced by its geometry, where right angles, large windows, and light colors predominate. The design plan was executed inside a building whose two levels are connected by an attractive metal and wood stairway. The richness and warmth of the interior mainly stems from the wood details and the finish. The upper level, containing the master bedroom, makes a connection between the interior and the exterior. The wood extends from the private area, passes through the large window, and continues along the terrace. In this very austere space, a low cement wall defines the bathroom area, linking it to the main area. The only piece of furniture in this space is the bed, which faces the exterior terrace.

House in Kuessnacht

› Samuel Lerch

Kuessnacht, Switzerland › 2003 › Photos © Bruno Helbling / zapaimages

☐ El arquitecto entiende esta casa como la estructura de un coche, en donde el concepto de lujo es el vacío más que el exceso de elementos en el interior del espacio. En este proyecto el principal ejercicio ha sido el de eliminar, más que el de añadir. La sobriedad del espacio resalta gracias a una geometría en la que predominan los ángulos rectos, los amplios ventanales y los colores claros. El programa de la vivienda se desarrolla en un volumen de

☐ Für den Architekten ist dieses Haus ein Skelett, das sich unter den Autos befindet, und in dem Luxus eher als Leere anstelle überladener Räume verstanden wird. Bei dieser Planung hat man mehr weggenommen als hinzugefügt. Die Schlichtheit der Räume wird durch eine Geometrie unterstrichen, in der die geraden Winkel, große Fenster und helle Farben vorherrschen. Die einzelnen Räume erstrecken sich über zwei Stockwerke, die durch

dos plantas unidas por una sugerente escalera de metal y madera. Este material es el principal detalle de acabado que otorga riqueza y calidez al interior. La parte superior, que alberga la habitación principal, vincula el interior con el exterior. La madera se extiende desde la zona privada hasta la terraza, atravesando el ventanal. En este espacio de gran sobriedad destaca el muro a media altura de cemento que define la zona de lavabos, vinculada al espacio principal. El único mobiliario de esta zona es la cama, ubicada frente a la terraza exterior.

eine schön gestaltete Treppe aus Metall und Holz verbunden sind. Dieses Material ist das wichtigste Gestaltungselement, das das Innere reich und warm wirken lässt. Im Obergeschoss befindet sich das Wohnzimmer, das eine Verbindung zwischen innen und außen herstellt. Das Element Holz erstreckt sich von den Privaträumen über das große Fenster bis zur Terrasse. In diesem sehr schlicht gehaltenen Raum hebt sich eine Zementmauer auf halber Höhe ab, die die Bereiche der Badezimmer definiert, die mit dem Hauptraum verbunden sind. Das einzige Möbelstück hier ist das Bett selbst, das sich gegenüber der Terrasse befindet.

› Ground floor

› Planta baja

› Erdgeschoss

› First floor

› Planta primera

› Erster Stock

0 2 4

> Second floor
> Planta segunda
> Zweiter Stock

1. What historical reference in particular inspires you when designing a residence?
   ¿Qué referente histórico en particular le sirve de fuente de inspiración a la hora de proyectar una vivienda?
   Welche historische Referenz dient Ihnen als Inspiration beim Entwurf eines Hauses?

2. What is the main factor taken into consideration when designing a residence?
   ¿Cuál es el principal factor determinante a la hora de diseñar una vivienda?
   Welche Rahmenbedingungen, bzw. Faktoren sind für Sie ausschlaggebend beim Konzipieren?

3. What room inside the home do you find most interesting to design?
   ¿Qué estancia de la vivienda encuentra usted más interesante para diseñar?
   Welchen Raum des Hauses finden Sie am spannendsten zu entwerfen?

4. What is your criteria for choosing materials and finishings in a particular room?
   ¿Cuál es su criterio a la hora de seleccionar los materiales y los acabados en esta estancia?
   Welche Kriterien wenden Sie bei der Entscheidung über Materialen und Oberflächen in diesem Raum an?

1. The straight-line style of the Bauhaus architects.

2. The design is determined by the future use of the space and by its surroundings.

3. The heart of the house, the place where people gather.

4. Light materials that are attractive and pleasing to the eye even after many years.

1. El estilo de líneas rectas de los arquitectos de la Bauhaus.

2. El espacio exterior existente y los futuros usos determinan el diseño.

3. El corazón de la casa, el centro de reunión social.

4. Materiales ligeros que resultan atractivos y agradables de ver incluso después de muchos años. La orientación natural de la luz, el juego cambiante de luces y sombras, que se continúa en la oscuridad con luz artificial.

1. Der geradlinige Stil der Bauhaus.Architekten.

2. Die Gestaltung wird von dem bereits existierenden Raum und der zukünftigen Nutzung bestimmt.

3. Das Herz des Hauses, der Ort, an dem sich die Menschen treffen.

4. Leichte Materialien, die sogar nach vielen Jahren noch angenehm und anziehend wirken.

Samuel Lerch was born in 1958, and received his architecture degree in 1980. During the first phase of his career he specialized in construction, working with several companies between 1981 and 1983. From 1984 to 1988 he was associated with various architectural and design offices, until he finally founded his own practice in Zurich in 1989. He mainly works on residential projects that involve new construction, but he also rehabilitates existing buildings, and does renovations and interior design.

Samuel Lerch nació en 1958 y se diplomó como arquitecto en 1980. En su primera fase de trabajo se centró en el campo de la construcción colaborando para varias empresas entre 1981 y 1983. Posteriormente, se dedicó a colaborar en varios despachos de arquitectura y diseño, entre 1984 y 1988, hasta fundar su propia oficina en Zurich, en 1989. Su trabajo se centra principalmente en proyectos de vivienda y comprende tanto proyectos de obra nueva como rehabilitaciones de edificios existentes, reformas y diseño de interiores.

Samuel Lerch wurde 1958 geboren und schloss 1980 sein Architekturstudium erfolgreich ab. In seiner ersten Arbeitsphase zwischen 1981 und 1983 arbeitete er für verschiedene Unternehmen im Bereich Konstruktion. Nachdem er dann zwischen 1984 und 1988 mit verschiedenen Architekturbüros zusammengearbeitet hatte, gründete er 1989 in Zürich sein eigenes Studio. Bei seiner Arbeit konzentriert er sich hauptsächlich auf Wohnhäuser, sowohl Neubauten als auch Umbauten bereits bestehender Gebäude, Renovierungen und Innenarchitektur.

□ A building that was abandoned for more than ten years served as the structural base for this project, which now contains three luxury apartments in the Islington neighborhood in Northwest London. An original aspect of this project is that all the units were individually designed to create a unique feeling in each through the use of light, color, and the layout of the space. Special attention was given to designing practical surroundings in the residence: large storage areas, intelligent lighting, sound systems, and bathrooms and kitchens equipped with the latest technical features. The lower apartments occupy a single level while the top one was designed to be spectacular with a double height ceiling. A large glass and steel canopy fills the entire ceiling and frames the view of the living room. The interior details and materials, dominated by stainless steel, wood, and glass, reinforce the impact of the space.

Shoreditch Conversion

› Gregory Phillips Architects

London, UK › 2002 › Photos © Paul Smoothy

☐ Un edificio abandonado durante más de diez años sirvió como estructura base para crear este proyecto de vivienda que alberga ahora tres residencias de lujo en el barrio de Islington, en la parte nordeste de Londres. Un aspecto original de este proyecto es que cada una de las unidades fue diseñada individualmente para lograr producir en cada caso una atmósfera propia a través de la luz, el color y la disposición del espacio. Se prestó especial

☐ Ein seit über zehn Jahren leer stehendes Gebäude war Gegenstand dieser Planung eines Wohnhauses, in dem drei Luxuswohnungen untergebracht sind. Es liegt im Nordosten Londons im Viertel Islington. Was dieses Gebäude sehr originell macht, ist die Tatsache, dass jede der Wohnungen individuell geplant wurde, um in jeder mithilfe des Lichtes, der Farben und der Anordnung der Räume eine eigene Atmosphäre zu schaffen. Besondere

atención en diseñar un entorno práctico para la vivienda: amplias zonas de almacenamiento, iluminación inteligente, equipos de sonido y baños y cocinas con la última tecnología incorporada. Las viviendas inferiores se plantean en una sola planta, mientras que la superior se diseñó como un volumen de doble altura de gran espectacularidad. Una gran marquesina de acero y cristal engloba la doble altura del espacio y enmarca la panorámica de la sala de estar de la vivienda. Los materiales y detalles interiores, en donde predomina el acero inoxidable, la madera y el cristal, acentúan la contundencia del espacio interior.

Aufmerksamkeit wurde beim Entwurf auf die praktische Umgebung der Wohnung gerichtet. So gibt es geräumige Aufbewahrungsbereiche, eine intelligente Beleuchtung, Tonsysteme, Bäder und Küchen, die mit den letzten technischen Neuheiten ausgestattet sind. Die Wohnungen der unteren Stockwerke liegen auf einer Etage, während die im letzten Stockwerk zweistöckig und besonders schön ist. Eine große Markise aus Stahl und Kristall umfasst die doppelte Höhe des Raumes und bildet einen Rahmen für das Wohnzimmer dieser Wohnung. Die Materialien und Elemente im Inneren, bei denen Edelstahl, Holz und Glas dominieren, unterstreichen noch die Wirkung der Räume.

0   2   4

› **Basement plan**

› Planta sótano

› Untergeschoss

› **Ground floor**

› Planta baja

› Erdegeschoss

› **First floor**

› Planta primera

› Erster Stock

› **Second floor**

› Planta segunda

› Zweiter Stock

> Third floor
> Planta tercera
> Dritter Stock

> Fourth floor
> Planta cuarta
> Vierter Stock

> Fifth floor
> Planta quinta
> Fünfter Stock

> Roof plan
> Planta de cubiertas
> Dachgrundriss

0 2 4

1. What historical reference in particular inspires you when designing a residence?

   ¿Qué referente histórico en particular le sirve de fuente de inspiración a la hora de proyectar una vivienda?

   Welche historische Referenz dient Ihnen als Inspiration beim Entwurf eines Hauses?

2. What is the main factor taken into consideration when designing a residence?

   ¿Cuál es el principal factor determinante a la hora de diseñar una vivienda?

   Welche Rahmenbedingungen, bzw. Faktoren sind für Sie ausschlaggebend beim Konzipieren?

3. What room inside the home do you find most interesting to design?

   ¿Qué estancia de la vivienda encuentra usted más interesante para diseñar?

   Welchen Raum des Hauses finden Sie am spannendsten zu entwerfen?

4. What is your criteria for choosing materials and finishings in a particular room?

   ¿Cuál es su criterio a la hora de seleccionar los materiales y los acabados en esta estancia?

   Welche Kriterien wenden Sie bei der Entscheidung über Materialen und Oberflächen in diesem Raum an?

---

1. A house should be a sanctuary and a place that works for the owners; thus for me it is a combination of a temple, a machine for living in and the best most luxurious hotel.

2. It is a question of meeting the needs of the client, making the spaces work for their lifestyle and creating elegance. We also look to create wonderful spaces that make the most of the features of the site or building.

3. The living room and kitchen have to allow for many functions to occur. They are used throughout the day in various ways. These spaces are a fascinating challenge to create elegance, comfort and function.

4. Beauty, practicality, longevity.

---

1. Una casa debería ser una especie de santuario y un lugar práctico para los propietarios; por este motivo, constituye para mí la combinación de un templo, un aparato para vivir y el hotel más lujoso.

2. Es cuestión de conocer las necesidades del cliente, hacer que los espacios resulten útiles para su estilo de vida y crear elegancia. Asimismo, intentamos diseñar espacios maravillosos que aprovechen al máximo las características del solar o del edificio.

3. La sala de estar y la cocina deben albergar muchas funciones, ya que se utilizan durante el día de diversas maneras. Estos espacios son especialmente fascinantes a la hora de crear ambientes elegantes, confortables y funcionales.

4. Belleza, funcionalidad y durabilidad.

---

1. Ein Haus sollte eine Art heiliger Ort, aber auch ein praktischer Ort für die Besitzer sein. Deshalb ist es eine Kombination aus Tempel, Wohnapparat und Luxushotel.

2. Man muss die Bedürfnisse des Kunden kennen, und nützliche Räume für seinen Lebensstil und gleichzeitig Eleganz schaffen. Wir versuchen auch wundervolle Räume zu gestalten, mit denen wir die Möglichkeiten des Grundstückes oder des Hauses voll ausschöpfen. Vielleicht große Fenster, um den Ausblick zu genießen oder Räume doppelter Höhe, die die wichtigen Aspekte des Gebäudes miteinander verbinden.

3. Das Wohnzimmer und die Küche müssen vielen Funktionen dienen, da sie im Laufe des Tages auf verschiedene Weise genutzt werden. Diese Räume sind besonders interessant bei der Gestaltung eleganter, komfortabler und funktioneller Wohnatmosphären.

4. Schönheit, Funktionalität und Dauerhaftigkeit.

Gregory Phillips Architects is a young firm based in London. It consists of Gregory Phillips, who worked with David Chipperfield, and two other architects — Jay Salero, who practiced at Foster and Partners for three years, and Cathy Curran, a collaborator of Richard Rogers for four years — who act as project directors. Phillips, who founded his own office in 1991, is a devotee of esthetics and modern technology, and of developing any project of any scale.

Gregory Phillips Architects es una firma joven con sede en Londres. El propio Gregory Phillips es parte integrante, quien trabajó con David Chipperfield, y otros dos arquitectos como directores de proyectos: Jay Salero, que trabajó en Foster and Partners durante tres años, y Cathy Curran, que colaboró con Richard Rogers durante cuatro años. Phillips, quien fundó su propia oficina en 1991, es un devoto de la estética y la tecnología moderna y en la creación de cualquier proyecto a cualquier escala.

Gregory Phillips Architects ist ein junges Architekturbüro mit Sitz in London. Hier arbeiten Gregory Phillips selbst, der auch mit David Chipperfield kollaboriert hatte, und weitere Architekten, die verschiedene Projektleitungen übernehmen, nämlich Jay Salero, der drei Jahre lang bei Foster and Partners arbeitete, und Cathy Curran, die vier Jahre mit Richard Rogers zusammenarbeitete. Phillips, der sein Unternehmen 1991 gründete, liebt die Ästhetik und moderne Technologie und er sieht es als eine Herausforderung an, jegliches Projekt jeder Größenordnung zu übernehmen.

☐ This residential project in Barcelona consisted of renovating the upper level of an old industrial building with a pitched roof. The original space had a large ground floor and a small top floor with access to a terrace. The primary objectives were to flood the space with natural light and to create spacious rooms. A large skylight was installed over the living and dining areas while other smaller openings were made to illuminate the bathrooms. The framework crossing the grand central skylight causes the light to reflect in several directions, creating a changing environment throughout the day. The layout of the space is organized around a furniture element that separates the night area from the day area. It does not reach as far as the ceiling or to the outside walls of the apartment, a feature that emphasizes the fluidity of the space. The piece serves as a shelf on the social side and as a closet on the private side. The communication between the sleeping area and the salon, or between the salon and the kitchen, is more flexible and striking because of the sliding doors.

Residence in Gracia

› Sandra Aparicio + Forteza Carbonell Associats

Barcelona, Spain › 2002 › Photos © Santiago Garcès

☐ El proyecto de esta vivienda consistió en la reforma de un ático, con cubierta a dos aguas, en un antiguo edificio industrial de Barcelona. El espacio original contaba con una amplia superficie en la planta baja y una pequeña planta superior que daba acceso a una terraza. El principal objetivo era el de inundar el espacio con luz natural y crear estancias muy amplias. Para lograrlo se creó un gran lucernario que marcara la zona de estar y comedor,

☐ Diese Wohnung entstand durch die Renovierung eines Penthouses mit Satteldach in einem alten Industriegebäude in Barcelona. Die Originalräume besaßen ein geräumiges Erdgeschoss und ein kleines Obergeschoss mit Zugang zur Terrasse. Vor allem wollte man viel Tageslicht in die Räume bringen und sie weitläufig wirken lassen. Dazu wurde ein großes Dachfenster eingebaut, das zu einem prägenden Element im

mientras que otras aberturas más pequeñas iluminaran los baños. Las intersecciones que atraviesan el gran lucernario central contribuyen a que la luz se refleje de diversas maneras y cree atmósferas variadas durante el día. El espacio se organiza a partir de un mueble central que separa la zona diurna de la nocturna y no llega a tocar el techo ni el perímetro de la vivienda, de esta manera ensalza la fluidez del espacio. El mueble funciona como estantería en la zona social y como armario para el ámbito privado. La relación entre la zona de dormir y el salón, o entre el salón y la cocina, se vuelve más flexible y contundente gracias a las puertas correderas.

Wohnzimmer und Esszimmer wurde. Die Helligkeit dringt durch kleinere Fenster in die Bäder ein. Die Schnittstellen, die sich durch das große zentrale Dachfenster ziehen, verursachen verschiedene Lichtreflexe, die die Stimmung in den Räumen im Laufe des Tages sehr verändern. Der Raum organisiert sich um ein zentrales Möbelstück herum, das die Bereiche für den Tag und die Nacht trennt und weder die Decke noch die Wände der Wohnung berührt, so dass der Raum sehr fließend wirkt. Zum Wohnbereich hin dient dieses Möbel als Regal, zu den Schlafzimmern hin als Schrank. Die Beziehung zwischen den Schlafzimmern und dem Wohnzimmern und zwischen dem Wohnzimmer und der Küche wird durch Schiebetüren noch flexibler und fließender.

0 2 4

› Plan
› Planta
› Grundriss

› Roof plan
› Planta de cubierta
› Dachgrundriss

0 1 2

› Sections
› Secciones
› Schnitte

1. What historical reference in particular inspires you when designing a residence?
   ¿Qué referente histórico en particular le sirve de fuente de inspiración a la hora de proyectar una vivienda?
   Welche historische Referenz dient Ihnen als Inspiration beim Entwurf eines Hauses?

2. What is the main factor taken into consideration when designing a residence?
   ¿Cuál es el principal factor determinante a la hora de diseñar una vivienda?
   Welche Rahmenbedingungen, bzw. Faktoren sind für Sie ausschlaggebend beim Konzipieren?

3. What room inside the home do you find most interesting to design?
   ¿Qué estancia de la vivienda encuentra usted más interesante para diseñar?
   Welchen Raum des Hauses finden Sie am spannendsten zu entwerfen?

4. What is your criteria for choosing materials and finishings in a particular room?
   ¿Cuál es su criterio a la hora de seleccionar los materiales y los acabados en esta estancia?
   Welche Kriterien wenden Sie bei der Entscheidung über Materialen und Oberflächen in diesem Raum an?

1. We find inspiration in different historical periods, probably because our projects are more related to interior design.

2. Fulfilling the functional requirements and the location of the project.

3. The living room is where people spend most of their time, so it is probably there that the overall feeling of the house can be summed up.

4. We usually choose three or four materials that are carried through all the rooms in the house. They always tend to be high quality materials.

1. Encontramos referencias en distintos momentos históricos, probablemente porque nuestros proyectos son más de interiorismo.

2. El programa funcional requerido y el lugar en el que esta se ubica.

3. El salón es el lugar en el que se acostumbra a estar más horas, en el que probablemente puedes sintetizar la atmósfera general de la vivienda.

4. Habitualmente decidimos tres o cuatro materiales y los repetimos en todas las estancias de la vivienda. Acostumbran a ser siempre materiales nobles.

1. Vielleicht finden wir deshalb zu verschiedenen Zeitpunkten der Geschichte Referenzen, weil unsere Projekte sich mehr mit der Innenarchitektur beschäftigen.

2. Das notwendige Wohnprogramm und der Standort.

3. Das Wohnzimmer ist der Ort, in dem man sich meistens mehr Stunden aufzuhalten pflegt, und in dem man die allgemeine Atmosphäre des Hauses oder der Wohnung zusammenfassen kann.

4. Normalerweise entscheiden wir uns für drei oder vier Materialien und wiederholen diese in allen Räumen der Wohnung. Wir arbeiten meist mit edlen Materialien.

Ignacio Forteza of Forteza Carbonell Associats, and Sandra Aparicio have collaborated on interior design projects since 1995. Forteza Carbonell Associats also does architectural design. Their work is based on respect and function, interpreting the needs of the client and trying to impart a magical sense to the spaces that will provoke thinking. The use of materials in their original form, and a careful execution of the construction is characteristic of their work.

Ignacio Forteza, del equipo Forteza Carbonell Associats, y Sandra Aparicio colaboran juntos desde 1995 en el campo del diseño interior. Asimismo, Forteza Carbonell Associats trabaja a su vez en el campo de la arquitectura. La labor que desarrollan parte del respeto y la funcionalidad del trabajo. Interpretan las necesidades del cliente e intentan aportar una mirada mágica a los espacios y volverlos sugerentes. Los rasgos característicos de sus obras son la utilización de materiales en estado primitivo y la cuidada ejecución en la edificación.

Ignacio Forteza von Forteza Carbonell Associats und Sandra Aparicio arbeiten schon seit 1995 bei der Gestaltung von Innenräumen zusammen. Forteza Carbonell Associats beschäftigt sich auch mit Architektur. Die Arbeitsphilosophie dieser Architekten stützt sich auf die Pfeiler Respekt und Funktionalität. Sie interpretieren die Bedürfnisse ihrer Kunden und versuchen die Räume magisch und suggestiv zu gestalten. Typisch für ihre Planungen ist die Verwendung von Materialien in ihrem ursprünglichen Zustand und eine sehr sorgfältiges Arbeiten beim Bau.

☐ This project consisted of a total renovation to convert an old 1980's building, used as a photography studio, into a residential complex. Although the building had no special architectural character, it did have a double structure that created different kinds of spaces in its interior. Some rooms had very high ceilings while others were of a conventional height. After removing the walls these variations resulted in areas with different floor and ceiling heights, which created an interesting layout. The architects always begin with the premise that a conversion not only means changing the use of a building, but also adapting it to create a new kind of space. In this sense they visualized the possibility of excavating and creating a patio around the ground floor, making it easier to use. This way they not only adapted the interior space, but the exterior experienced a dramatic transformation as well. During the renovation's design process, the architects tried to employ the same methods that are normally used for new construction. This entailed the careful analysis of the location's characteristics and an attempt at maximizing the use of the building through intelligent design.

Motoazabu Housing Complex

› Yasushi Ikeda, Akiko Kokubun / IKDS

Minatoku, Tokyo, Japan › 2003 › Photos © Toshiharu Kitajima

☐ El objetivo de este proyecto fue lograr la renovación integral de un antiguo edificio de la década de 1980, utilizado como estudio de fotografía, y convertirlo en un complejo de viviendas. Aunque el edificio no tenía ninguna característica arquitectónica especial, sí contaba con una doble estructura que generaba diferentes tipos de espacios en su interior. Había habitaciones que tenían techos muy altos, mientras que otras, una altura conven-

☐ Hier wurde der gesamte Umbau eines ehemaligen Fotostudios aus den Achtzigerjahren in einen Wohnungskomplex geplant. Obwohl das Gebäude keine spezifischen, architektonischen Kennzeichen aufwies, gab es dennoch eine doppelte Struktur, durch die verschiedene Raumtypen im Inneren entstanden. Es gab besonders hohe und normal hohe Räume. Nach dem Abriss der Wände entstanden also Räumlichkeiten, in denen die

cional. Tras derribar las paredes, estas diferencias crearon espacios en donde los suelos o los techos varían de altura y muestran, por tanto, un interesante juego interior. Los arquitectos parten de la base de que una conversión no sólo es cambiar el uso de un edificio, sino adaptarlo para crear un nuevo tipo de espacio. En este sentido, visualizaron la posibilidad de excavar y crear un patio en torno a la planta baja para que esta pudiera ser aprovechada. De este modo, no sólo se adecuó el espacio interior, sino que el volumen exterior sufrió una dramática transformación. En el proceso de diseño de la reforma se intentó emplear el mismo método que se utiliza normalmente para una obra nueva, es decir, analizar las características del lugar en detalle y tratar de maximizar el uso del edificio por medio de un diseño inteligente.

Böden oder die Decken verschiedene Höhen hatten, was eine interessante Wirkung erzielte. Die Architekten gingen davon aus, dass man durch einen Umbau nicht nur die Nutzungsart eines Gebäudes verändert, sondern dass man eine neue Wohnlandschaft schafft. So kamen sie zum Beispiel auf die Idee, einen Hof um das Erdgeschoss anzulegen, damit man dieses besser ausnutzen konnte. Also wurde nicht nur das Innere umgebaut, sondern auch von außen wurden große Veränderungen vorgenommen. Bei der Umgestaltung des Gebäudes versuchte man die gleiche Methode zu benutzen, die normalerweise bei einem Neubau angewendet wird. Man analysierte also die Eigenschaften des Bauplatzes genau und versuchte, dem Gebäude durch intelligente Gestaltung eine größtmögliche Nutzbarkeit zu geben.

› Basement

› Planta sótano

› Untergeschoss

› Ground floor

› Planta baja

› Erdegeschoss

› First floor

› Planta primera

› Erster Stock

> Second floor
> Planta segunda
> Zweiter Stock

0 2 4

> Section
> Sección
> Schnitt

1. What historical reference in particular inspires you when designing a residence?
¿Qué referente histórico en particular le sirve de fuente de inspiración a la hora de proyectar una vivienda?
Welche historische Referenz dient Ihnen als Inspiration beim Entwurf eines Hauses?

2. What is the main factor taken into consideration when designing a residence?
¿Cuál es el principal factor determinante a la hora de diseñar una vivienda?
Welche Rahmenbedingungen, bzw. Faktoren sind für Sie ausschlaggebend beim Konzipieren?

3. What room inside the home do you find most interesting to design?
¿Qué estancia de la vivienda encuentra usted más interesante para diseñar?
Welchen Raum des Hauses finden Sie am spannendsten zu entwerfen?

4. What is your criteria for choosing materials and finishings in a particular room?
¿Cuál es su criterio a la hora de seleccionar los materiales y los acabados en esta estancia?
Welche Kriterien wenden Sie bei der Entscheidung über Materialen und Oberflächen in diesem Raum an?

1. Ways that the nature has been incorporated in architectures in the past is the historical reference that inspires us the most such as use of natural light and wind.

2. The majority of our work has been residences in urban area. Thus, the main factor that is taken consideration when designing a residence is how we can incorporate a life style of a resident to town space.

3. Our interest expands beyond designing a particular room. We are rather interested in continuity of rooms and spaces of a house.

4. We do not choose materials not only by their looks and colors but also by their touch, feel, acoustic quality, and combination of materials.

1. La referencia histórica que más nos inspira es la forma en la que la naturaleza se ha incorporado a la arquitectura en el pasado, por ejemplo, con la incorporación del viento y la luz natural.

2. La mayoría de nuestros trabajos han sido residencias urbanas. Por esta razón, nuestra mayor preocupación cuando diseñamos un espacio consiste en intentar incorporar el estilo de vida de sus habitantes en el espacio urbano.

3. Nuestros intereses se extienden más allá del diseño de una habitación en particular. Estamos más interesados en la continuidad entre las habitaciones y los espacios de la vivienda.

4. No elegimos los materiales solamente por su aspecto y color, sino por su tacto, calidad acústica y la combinación con los otros materiales.

1. Die historische Referenz, die uns am meisten inspiriert, ist die Art und Weise, wie man die Natur in die Architektur der Vergangenheit integriert hat, zum Beispiel, wie mit dem Wind oder dem Tageslicht umgegangen wurde.

2. Die meisten unserer Arbeiten sind städtische Wohnhäuser. Deshalb ist es für uns bei der Gestaltung eines Raumes sehr wichtig, den Lebensstil seiner Bewohner in die städtische Umgebung zu integrieren.

3. Unsere Interessen gehen weit über die Gestaltung eines speziellen Raumes hinaus. Uns interessiert die Kontinuität zwischen den Zimmern und Räumen einer Wohnung.

4. Wir wählen die Materialien nicht allein aufgrund ihres Aussehens und ihrer Farbe aus, sondern auch danach, wie sie sich anfühlen, nach ihren akustischen Eigenschaften und wie sie sich mit anderen Materialien kombinieren lassen.

Yasushi Ikeda was born in 1961 in Fukuoka. He studied in the Architecture School at the University of Tokyo and worked in the architectural office of Maki and Associates (1987-1995). Later, he established Ikeda Design Studio. Since 1996 he is an assistant professor in the School of Environmental Information in Keio University.
Akiko Kokubun was born in 1965 in Tokyo. She studied in the Architecture School at the University of Tokyo and worked in the architectural office of Maki and Associates (1988-1997). In 1997 she joined the Ikeda Kokubun Design Studio.

Yasushi Ikeda nació en Fukuoka en 1961. Estudió en el departamento de arquitectura de la Universidad de Tokio y trabajó en la oficina de arquitectura Maki and Associates (1987-1995). Posteriomente, estableció Ikeda Design Studio. Desde 1996 es profesor asistente en la Escuela de Información Mediambiental, en la Universidad de Keio.
Akiko Kokubun nació en Tokio en 1965. Estudió en la facultad de arquitectura de la Universidad de Tokio y trabajó en la oficina de arquitectura Maki and Associates (1988-1997). En 1997 se asoció a Ikeda Kokubun Design Studio.

Yasushi Ikeda kam 1961 in Fukuoka zur Welt. Er studierte Architektur an der Universität von Tokio und arbeitete in dem Unternehmen Maki and Associates (1987-1995). Später gründete er Ikeda Design Studio. Seit 1996 ist er assistierender Professor an der Fakultät für Umweltinformation der Keio Universität.
Akiko Kokubun kam 1965 in Tokio zur Welt. Sie studierte Architektur an der Universität von Tokio und arbeitete in dem Unternehmen Maki and Associates (1988-1997). 1997 wurde sie Mitbegründerin des Kokubun Design Studios.

The history of this project began with the need to cover the top floor of this building in order to protect the lower levels from the elements. The resulting space was later occupied by separate, individual structures. In their approach to the renovation project the architects used this concept as a point of departure to create a residence based on minimal units that were developed according to a mutual relationship. The placement of the units was based on geometric shapes that break up the building's existing straight lines. This manipulation of form helps direct the eye towards distant views, beyond the surrounding neighbors. The interior units can be expanded and adapted according to specific needs using textile panels that slide on rails. These elements can also be folded so that the spaces can almost entirely be integrated. The roof extends beyond the sides of the building to create overhanging glass projections, which show the interior work while covering projections from the lower floors of the building.

Rooftop

› Holodeck.at

Vienna, Austria › 2002 › Photos © Veronika Hofinger

☐ La historia de este proyecto comienza con la necesidad de cubrir la última planta de este edificio con el fin de proteger las plantas inferiores de las condiciones climáticas. El espacio resultante fue posteriormente ocupado por elementos concretos e individuales. Al abordar el proyecto de reforma, los arquitectos tomaron este concepto como punto de partida para la creación de una vivienda basada en unidades mínimas que se desarrollan entre sí.

☐ Die Grundlage dieser Planung war die Notwendigkeit, das Dach eines letzten Stockwerkes zu decken, um die unteren Stockwerke vor Wettereinflüssen zu schützen. Der dadurch entstandene Raum wurde allmählich von einzelnen, individuellen Elementen eingenommen. Die Architekten betrachteten dieses Renovierungsprojekt als Ausgangspunkt für die Erschaffung eines Wohnraumes, der auf minimalen Einheiten basiert, die sich gemeinsam

La disposición de las unidades parte de una geometría que rompe con las líneas ortogonales del edificio existente. Con este gesto formal se logra conducir la mirada hacia panorámicas muy lejanas, por encima del vecindario circundante. Las unidades interiores se pueden ampliar y adaptar según el uso específico gracias a paneles textiles que se deslizan sobre rieles. Estos elementos pueden también ser plegados y lograr así que la integración de las unidades sea prácticamente total. La cubierta se extiende por fuera de los límites de la vivienda en forma de voladizos de cristal, que evidencian la intervención interior y cubren las proyecciones del volumen del edificio en plantas inferiores.

entwickeln. Die Anordnung der Teile geht von einer Geometrie aus, die die rechtwinkligen Linien des existierenden Gebäudes bricht. Mit dieser formalen Geste wird der Blick auf das weit entfernte Panorama gelenkt, über den umgebenden Gebäuden gelegen. Die inneren Einheiten können mithilfe von Stoffpaneelen, die auf Führungen verschoben werden, für die jeweilige Nutzung erweitert oder verändert werden. Diese Elemente können auch gefaltet werden, so dass die Einheiten praktisch zu einem einzigen Raum werden können. Das Dach erstreckt sich außerhalb der Wohnung in Form von gläsernen Vorsprüngen, und zeigt somit die äußeren und inneren Eingriffe und deckt gleichzeitig die Wohnung und die unteren Stockwerke des Gebäudes.

› Ground floor

› Planta baja

› Erdegeschoss

› Section

› Sección

› Schnitt

0   1   2

> Model
> Modelo
> Modell

1. What historical reference in particular inspires you when designing a residence?
¿Qué referente histórico en particular le sirve de fuente de inspiración a la hora de proyectar una vivienda?
Welche historische Referenz dient Ihnen als Inspiration beim Entwurf eines Hauses?

2. What is the main factor taken into consideration when designing a residence?
¿Cuál es el principal factor determinante a la hora de diseñar una vivienda?
Welche Rahmenbedingungen, bzw. Faktoren sind für Sie ausschlaggebend beim Konzipieren?

3. What room inside the home do you find most interesting to design?
¿Qué estancia de la vivienda encuentra usted más interesante para diseñar?
Welchen Raum des Hauses finden Sie am spannendsten zu entwerfen?

4. What is your criteria for choosing materials and finishings in a particular room?
¿Cuál es su criterio a la hora de seleccionar los materiales y los acabados en esta estancia?
Welche Kriterien wenden Sie bei der Entscheidung über Materialen und Oberflächen in diesem Raum an?

---

1. The continuity and complexity of spaces and the social interactivity in the historical 'medina' as well as the principle of the courtyard house.

2. The adaption of the program 'housing' to the complexity of the clients desires combined with the particularities of the site.

3. The continuum of spaces and their flexible arrangement following the functional and emotional demands of the client.

4. To emphasize the conceptual idea.

---

1. La continuidad y complejidad de los espacios y la interactividad social en la histórica medina como concepto de casa ajardinada.

2. La adaptación del programa a la complejidad de los deseos de los clientes combinada con las particularidades del solar.

3. La continuidad de espacios y su distribución flexible siguiendo las demandas funcionales y emocionales del cliente.

4. Acentuar la idea abstracta.

---

1. Die Kontinuität und die Vielschichtigkeit der Räume und die soziale Dialogfähigkeit in den historischen, arabischen Altstädten als das Konzept eines Hauses mit Garten.

2. Die Anpassung der Wohnprogramme an die Vielschichtigkeit der Wünsche der Kunden in Kombination mit den Eigenschaften des Grundstückes.

3. Die Kontinuität der Räume und die flexible Verteilung, die den funktionellen und emotionalen Wünschen des Kunden entspricht.

4. Die abstrakte Idee unterstreichen.

Holodeck.at is a design office founded in 1998 by Marlies Breuss, Michael Ogertsching and Susanne Schmall. She left the firm at the beginning of 2001, gaining additional experience at studios in Los Angeles, Barcelona, and Tokyo. Her philosophy is based on a conceptual and logical plan that focuses on restructuring projects and developing specific functions. Holodeck.at creates the design tools required for their projects by collecting and researching information on the particular location.

Holodeck.at es una oficina de diseño fundada en 1998 por Marlies Breuss, Michael Ogertsching y Susanne Schmall. A principios de 2001 Susanne Schmall deja la firma, y su experiencia se enriquece con estudios en Los Ángeles, Barcelona y Tokio. Su filosofía parte de un esquema conceptual y programático en donde se ocupa principalmente de la reestructuración de programas y el desarrollo de funciones específicas. Holodeck.at obtiene las herramientas de diseño para sus encargos gracias al almacenamiento y a la filtración de informaciones de un lugar concreto.

Holodeck.at ist ein Architekturbüro, das von Marlies Breuss, Michael Ogertsching und Susanne Schmall 1998 gegründet wurde. Susanne Schmall verließ die Firma 2001. Die Architekten haben durch Studien in Los Angeles, Barcelona und Tokio Erfahrung gesammelt. Die Unternehmensphilosophie beruht auf einem konzeptuellen und programmatischen Schema, hauptsächlich widmet man sich der Neustrukturierung von Wohnräumen und der Entwicklung spezifischer Funktionen. Durch das Speichern und Filtern von Informationen über den Standort werden die Gestaltungswerkzeuge für die einzelnen Aufträge geschaffen.

☐ The location of the Ray 1 project, on the top floor of a 1960's office building in the center of Vienna's fourth district, served as a reference and an inspiration for the design of the project. The architect's design, which inevitably had to take into account the strict regulations regarding the coverings of buildings, did not fit into the typical mold, but was approached as a reinterpretation of these kinds of regulations. In order to apply the design concept, a steel skeleton was used to evenly distribute the load on the building's original structure. The gable carries the main weight while the other metal parts act as frames for the glass covering. The result is surprisingly light and creates a structure that is particularly interesting in relation to the surrounding urban setting. The form of the structure itself, as well as the permanent relationship with the surrounding landscape, creates a dynamic atmosphere in the interior and an opportunity to experience the outside from terraces or through large openings.

Ray 1

› Delugan_Meissl

Vienna, Austria › 2003 › Photos © Rupert Steiner

La ubicación del Ray 1, en la última planta de un edificio de oficinas de la década de 1960, y en el corazón del cuarto distrito de Viena, sirve como referente y estímulo para el desarrollo del proyecto. El diseño, que inevitablemente debía conciliar las estrictas regulaciones con respecto a las cubiertas de edificios, no cae en los tópicos encasillamientos, sino que se plantea como una reinterpretación de este tipo de regulaciones. Para poder

Der Standort des Projektes Ray 1 im obersten Stockwerk eines Bürogebäudes aus den Sechzigerjahren, inmitten des vierten Bezirks von Wien, diente als Referenzpunkt und Inspiration für Durchführung des Projektes. Bei der Gestaltung konnten die strengen Verordnungen für die Gestaltung der Dächer nicht umgangen werden. Diese werden jedoch nicht als Einschränkungen aufgefasst, sondern sie werden einfach

trasladar el concepto de diseño a la estructura original del edificio, se optó por un esqueleto de acero que permite distribuir las cargas de una manera homogénea a los muros del edificio. Las cargas principales las recibe el hastial, mientras que los demás elementos metálicos sirven como marcos para un envoltorio de cristal. El resultado es de una ligereza sorprendente y crea un objeto de particular interés en relación con el entorno urbano más inmediato. La propia forma de la estructura así como la permanente relación con el paisaje circundante crean una atmósfera dinámica en su interior y una oportunidad para experimentar el exterior a modo de terrazas o grandes aberturas.

auf kreative Weise neu interpretiert. Um das Designkonzept auf die Originalstruktur des Gebäudes übertragen zu können, wurde ein Stahlskelett gewählt, über das die Lasten gleichmäßig auf die Mauern des Gebäudes übertragen werden. Die Hauptlasten werden von der Seitenwand getragen, während die übrigen Elemente aus Metall als Rahmen für die Hülle aus Glas dienen. Das Ergebnis wirkt überraschend leicht und es entstand ein Objekt, das in seiner unmittelbaren Umgebung sehr interessant wirkt. Die Form der Struktur selbst und die ständige Beziehung zu der umgebenden Landschaft schaffen eine dynamische Atmosphäre im Inneren und geben die Möglichkeit, außen mithilfe von Terrassen und großen Öffnungen zu experimentieren.

› **Elevations**
› Alzados
› Aufrisse

0 2 4

› **First floor**
› Planta primera
› Erster Stock

› **Second floor**
› Planta segunda
› Zweiter Stock

› **Sections**
› Secciones
› Schnitte

› Axonometry

› Axonometría

› Axonometrie

› Transversal section

› Sección transversal

› Querschnitt

1. What historical reference in particular inspires you when designing a residence?
¿Qué referente histórico en particular le sirve de fuente de inspiración a la hora de proyectar una vivienda?
Welche historische Referenz dient Ihnen als Inspiration beim Entwurf eines Hauses?

2. What is the main factor taken into consideration when designing a residence?
¿Cuál es el principal factor determinante a la hora de diseñar una vivienda?
Welche Rahmenbedingungen, bzw. Faktoren sind für Sie ausschlaggebend beim Konzipieren?

3. What room inside the home do you find most interesting to design?
¿Qué estancia de la vivienda encuentra usted más interesante para diseñar?
Welchen Raum des Hauses finden Sie am spannendsten zu entwerfen?

4. What is your criteria for choosing materials and finishings in a particular room?
¿Cuál es su criterio a la hora de seleccionar los materiales y los acabados en esta estancia?
Welche Kriterien wenden Sie bei der Entscheidung über Materialen und Oberflächen in diesem Raum an?

---

1. The architecture of Oscar Niemeyer and John Lautner.

2. In our concepts a building is always conceived as one aspect of something greater as existing within a spatial context. The design has its starting point in the genius loci.

3. A combination of living room and kitchen – we find it highly interesting how rooms interact with each other and how we could achieve the interior space as a flowing internal continuum whose various functional areas are defined by different floor levels, zones, or niches without using spatial or visual separators.

4. The materials we choose reflect and support the specific demanded use of each particular room and their haptic dimension is very important to us. In most cases we use materials in their original colour in order to give a starting point for an individual colourful occupation.

---

1. La arquitectura de Oscar Niemeyer y John Lautner.

2. En nuestros conceptos, un edificio siempre se concibe tanto como un elemento dentro de algo más grande que como pieza existente en un contexto espacial. El diseño tiene su punto de partida en el espíritu del lugar.

3. La combinación de sala de estar y cocina. Encontramos muy interesante el modo en que las diferentes habitaciones interactúan entre sí y cómo podemos conseguir que el espacio interior sea continuo, fluido y cuyas distintas áreas estén definidas por pavimentos, zonas o aberturas a diferentes niveles, sin necesidad de utilizar divisiones espaciales o visuales.

4. Los materiales que elegimos reflejan y acentúan el uso específico de cada habitación y su dimensión táctil es muy importante para nosotros. En la mayoría de los casos utilizamos los materiales con su color original con el fin de crear un punto de partida para una ocupación individual.

---

1. Die Architektur von Oscar Niemeyer und John Lautner.

2. Es ist unsere Auffassung, dass ein Gebäude immer als ein Element innerhalb einer existierenden, größeren Einheit in einem räumlichen Kontextes entworfen wird. Der Ausgangspunkt für die Gestaltung ist der Geist, der an dem Ort herrscht.

3. Eine Kombination von Wohnzimmer und Küche finden wir sehr interessant, da hier die verschiedenen Räume miteinander in Beziehung stehen. So wird ein durchgehender, fließender innerer Raum geschaffen, dessen verschiedenen Bereiche durch die Fußböden und Zonen oder Öffnungen auf verschiedener Höhe definiert sind, ohne dass dazu räumliche oder visuelle teilende Elemente notwendig sind.

4. Die von uns ausgewählten Materialien spiegeln die spezifische Nutzung jedes Zimmer wieder und verstärken sie. Die taktile Dimension ist uns sehr wichtig. In den meisten Fällen verwenden wir Materialien, ohne ihre Farbe zu verändern, um so einen Ausgangspunkt für eine individuelle Besetzung zu schaffen.

Elke Delugan-Meissl (Linz, Austria) and Roman Delugan (Merano, Italy) joined to found their own architectural office in 1993. If there is a principle that guides their design method it would probably be the landscape. For them, a building is always seen as another aspect of something much larger that forms part of a spatial context, and not just a single structure. The design of each element is approached as a synthesis of the setting, while attempting to contribute something that would complement it. Their work encompasses a wide range of residential projects.

Elke Delugan-Meissl (Linz, Austria) y Roman Delugan (Merano, Italia) se asociaron y fundaron su propio despacho de arquitectura en 1993. Si existiese un principio que guiara su método de diseño, sería probablemente el concepto de paisaje. Para ellos un edificio siempre está concebido como un aspecto más de algo mucho más grande que forma parte de un contexto espacial y no como una estructura solitaria. El diseño de cada elemento se plantea como una síntesis del entorno al tiempo que pretende contribuir a complementarlo. Su obra comprende una variada gama de proyectos residenciales.

Elke Delugan-Meissl (Linz, Österreich) und Roman Delugan (Meran, Italien) gründeten 1993 gemeinsam ein Architekturstudio. Falls es ein Prinzip gäbe, nach dem sich ihre Designmethode richtet, so wäre dies wahrscheinlich die Landschaft. Für diese Architekten ist ein Gebäude immer ein Aspekt einer größeren Einheit. Es gehört in einen räumlichen Kontext und ist keine einsame Struktur. Die Gestaltung jedes Elementes wird als die Synthese der Umgebung aufgefasst; gleichzeitig soll die Umgebung ergänzt werden. Sie haben bereits zahlreiche Projekte für Wohnanlagen verwirklicht.

□ This project consisted of enlarging seven units in an existing residential complex. Five of the units are arrayed in a long building while the other two are independent structures around an open patio. The model of the residences is based on the original plan, consisting of three levels inside each residence. The interrelated and open floor plan allows for a variety of uses. The connection between the spaces is emphasized by the double-height ceiling, while their close relationship to the exterior is enhanced by the large windows that open to each unit's small private garden. The old industrial lofts not only inspired the floor plan and the use of the space, they also served as a reference when the time came to select the materials and finishes. Wood, metal, brick, and glass are predominant, and the materials are always left exposed to impart an industrial character to the interior of each living space.

Bay Cities Lofts: Phase II
› Mark Mack Architects

Venice, CA, USA › 2003 › Photos © Undine Pröhl

☐ Este proyecto consistió en la ampliación de siete unidades de vivienda en un complejo residencial ya existente. Cinco de las unidades se agruparon en un edifico longitudinal, mientras que las otras dos se proyectaron como volúmenes independientes en torno a un patio abierto. La tipología de las viviendas está basada en el proyecto original y plantea una solución en vertical, con tres niveles en el interior de cada residencia. Los

☐ Dieses Projekt besteht in der Erweiterung von sieben Wohnungen in einem bereits existierenden Gebäude. Fünf dieser Wohnungen liegen in einem längs verlaufenden Gebäude, die anderen beiden sind unabhängige Bauten um einen offenen Hof. Die Wohnungen wurden im gleichen Stil wie das Originalgebäude gestaltet. Es wurde eine vertikale Lösung vorgeschlagen, bei der in jedem Wohnhaus drei Ebenen vorgesehen sind. Die offenen, mit-

espacios, abiertos y relacionados entre sí permiten ser aprovechados de diversas maneras. El vínculo entre los espacios, así como la estrecha relación con el exterior, se ensalza con la doble altura lograda en el interior y los amplios ventanales que se abren a los pequeños jardines privados de cada unidad. La inspiración en los antiguos lofts industriales ha servido no sólo para configurar la distribución y el uso del espacio, sino como referente a la hora de escoger los materiales y los acabados. Predomina el uso de la madera, el ladrillo, el metal y el cristal, que se trabajan siempre a la vista e imprimen un carácter industrial en el interior de cada vivienda.

einander verbundenen Räume können auf verschiedene Weise benutzt werden. Die Verbindung zwischen den Räumen und die enge Verbindung mit dem Äußeren wird noch durch die doppelte Höhe und die großen Fenster unterstrichen, die zu den kleinen Privatgärten jedes Wohnhauses zeigen. Sowohl die Verteilung und die Nutzung der Räume als auch die Auswahl der Materialien und Gestaltungselemente ist vom Stil alter Fabriketagen inspiriert. Hauptsächlich werden Holz, Ziegelstein, Metall und Glas verwendet. Diese Materialien sind immer sichtbar, was den industriellen Charakter im Innenausbau der Häuser unterstreicht.

0 2 4

› Ground floor

› Planta baja

› Erdegeschoss

› First floor

› Planta primera

› Erster Stock

› Second floor

› Planta segunda

› Zweiter Stock

> Transversal section
> Sección transversal
> Querschnitt

Mark Mack, along with his former partner Andrew Batey, earned his reputation as an architect in California mainly for his single-family home and villa designs in the early 1980's. He established his own office in San Francisco in 1984 and then moved to Venice, California in 1993. His approach to design is influenced by his academic work and restless curiosity. He was a professor in the School of Architecture at the University of California, Los Angeles. He was also a cofounder of Archetype Magazine and has contributed numerous articles to different magazines.

Mark Mack, junto a su antiguo socio Andrew Batey, se ha ganado su reputación como arquitecto en California principalmente por el diseño de villas y casas unifamiliares al inicio de la década de 1980. Estableció su propia oficina en San Francisco en 1984 y posteriormente se desplazó a Venice, California, en 1993. Su acercamiento al diseño está influenciado por sus inquietudes y su trabajo académico. Fue profesor de la Escuela de Arquitectura en la Universidad de California, Los Ángeles; asimismo fue cofundador de la revista Archetype Magazine y colaborador en numerosos artículos en diversas publicaciones.

Mark Mack begann seine Karriere Anfang der Achtzigerjahre mit der Planung von Einfamilienhäusern und Villen in Kalifornien zusammen mit seinem ehemaligen Teilhaber Andrew Batey. 1984 gründete er in San Francisco sein eigenes Unternehmen, das er 1993 nach Venice, Kalifornien, verlegte. Seine Interessen und seine akademische Arbeit beeinflussen stark seinen Gestaltungsstil. Er war Professor am Fachbereich Architektur der Universität von Kalifornien in Los Angeles. Ebenso ist er Mitbegründer der Zeitschrift Archetype Magazine, in der er zahlreiche Artikel veröffentlicht hat.

APARTMENTS

APARTAMENTOS / WOHNUNGEN

☐ This luxury apartment in the corner of the 49th floor of a building located on New York's Fifth Avenue has impressive views of Rockefeller Center and Midtown Manhattan. The clients, a German industrial magnate and his wife, envisioned an apartment characterized by light and spatial harmony that would be an urban refuge during their frequent visits to the city. The design of the interior renovation proposed minimal construction with a fluid integration between the different computerized systems to create an ideal setting for modern living. The design concept consisted of a light, crystal-clear space that functioned as an observatory of the metropolitan collage. The audiovisual system is contained in a structure that acts as the pivot point for the distribution of the main living and dining areas and the master bedroom. The atmosphere of the interior is created with several luxury materials and a basic palette dominated by white plaster, marble from Yugoslavia, and translucent crystal. A glass wall formed by two white enameled panels illuminated from below separates the kitchen from the dining area. The design balances the use of light, the forms, and the materials and allows them to co-exist in harmony in this Minimalist environment.

Olympic Tower Residence

› Gabellini Associates

New York, NY, USA › 2003 › Photos © Paul Warchol

☐ Este lujoso apartamento en la esquina de la planta 49 de un edificio ubicado en la Quinta Avenida de Nueva York cuenta con impresionantes visuales del Rockefeller Center y el Midtown de Manhattan. Los clientes, un magnate industrial alemán y su esposa, imaginaban una vivienda marcada por la claridad y la armonía espacial como refugio urbano a sus frecuentes visitas a la ciudad. El proyecto de reforma interior propone una

☐ Von diesem luxuriösen Appartement auf der Ecke eines 49. Stockwerks in einem Gebäude an der 5th Avenue von New York aus hat man einen überwältigenden Blick auf das Rockefeller Center und Midtown Manhattan. Die Kunden sind ein deutscher Industriemagnat und seine Ehefrau. Sie wünschten sich eine Wohnung, die von Klarheit und räumlicher Harmonie geprägt ist, und ihnen als Zufluchtsort bei ihren häufigen Besuchen in dieser

construcción minimalista en el que existe una integración fluida entre los diferentes sistemas inteligentes para producir un interior ideal para la vida moderna. El concepto de diseño propone crear un volumen cristalino y ligero que hace de observatorio al collage metropolitano. En un volumen se centralizan los sistemas audiovisuales y sirve de punto articulador para organizar las áreas de estar, comedor y habitación principal. La atmósfera interior está compuesta por una serie de materiales lujosos y una paleta elemental en donde predominan el blanco del yeso, el mármol de origen yugoslavo y el cristal translúcido. Una pared de cristal, formada por dos láminas esmaltadas blancas e iluminadas por la parte baja, divide la cocina del comedor. El diseño conjuga la utilización de la luz, las formas y los materiales para que coexistan armónicamente en este entorno minimalista.

Stadt dienen sollte. Die Gestaltung der Räume ist sehr minimalistisch und es findet eine fließende Integration zwischen verschiedenen, intelligenten Systemen statt, um eine ideale Umgebung für das moderne Leben zu schaffen. Die Gestalter schlugen kristallartige, leicht wirkende Räume vor, die zu einer Art Observatorium der Großstadt-Collage werden. In einem Raum befinden sich die audiovisuellen Systeme, von hier aus werden die Bereiche für das Wohnen, Essen und Schlafen organisiert. Die Atmosphäre ist von luxuriösen Materialien geprägt, die Farbpalette reicht vom Weiß des Gipses über die Töne des jugoslawischen Marmors bis zum durchsichtigen Glas. Eine Glaswand, die von zwei weiß emaillierten und von unten beleuchteten Platten gebildet wird, trennt die Küche vom Speisezimmer. Die Gestaltung spielt mit dem Licht, den Formen und den Materialien, damit sie sich harmonisch in diese minimalistische Umgebung einpassen.

› Plan

› Planta

› Grundriss

After finishing his studies at the Rhode Island School of Design in 1980 and complementing them at the Architectural Association of London, Michael Gabellini founded Gabellini Associates en 1991. Gabellini is known for his luxurious, elegant designs in which space and light are the main components. He has designed several boutiques for the most prestigious companies of the fashion world. His studies in art led him to carry out several projects for galleries and museums. In residential design he uses an esthetic that mixes the sophisticated and the casual to create a comfortable environment.

Después de estudiar arquitectura en la Escuela de Diseño de Rhode Island en 1980 y de haberlos complementado en la Architectural Association de Londres, Michael Gabellini fundó la firma Gabellini Associates en 1991. Gabellini es conocido por su diseño lujoso y elegante, donde la luz y el espacio son los principales materiales. En el campo de la moda ha diseñando varias boutiques para las más prestigiosas firmas. Su investigación en el arte lo ha llevado a realizar varios proyectos para museos y galerías. En el diseño de residencias utiliza una estética que mezcla sofisticación y casualidad para crear un entorno confortable.

Nach dem Michael Gabellini 1980 sein Architekturstudium an der Rhode Island School of Design abgeschlossen hatte, und sich an der Architectural Association in London weitergebildet hatte, gründete er 1991 Gabellini Associates. Gabellini ist für luxuriöse, elegante und elementaren Entwürfe bekannt, in denen Licht und Raum die wichtigsten Elemente sind. Aufgrund seines Interesses für die moderne Kunst hat er auch verschiedene Projekte für Museen und Galerien durchgeführt. Die von ihm gestalteten Wohnungen zeichnen dadurch aus, dass sie Edles mit spontaneren Elementen verbinden.

The architects describe this project as two halves that had functioned independently, which were combined to form a large and light-filled single unit. There were no restrictions other than the need for two bedrooms, so the architects designed a showcase that spanned the length of the house. The building was stripped to its foundation, and a long axis was created in the upper floor to articulate the different spaces in the residence. A double high gallery connected the two levels, which before were completely isolated from each other. An elegant metal stairway that looks like a piece of sculpture was added to the gallery, separating the salon from the library. The few colors and materials, separated from each other, enhance this sense of space. The floor of the more public lower level is made of sandstone, while the floor of the upper level, where the private rooms are located, is covered with wood parquet. The beige tone of the walls, halfway between the color of the stone and that of the wood, creates a monolithic effect of great tranquility.

House T

› Frei Architekten

Kloten, Switzerland › 2000 › Photos © Bruno Helbling / zapaimages

☐ Los arquitectos describen el proyecto como dos mitades, que funcionaban de forma independiente, y se unieron para formar una sola vivienda, amplia y luminosa. Aparte del requerimiento de dos dormitorios, no había ninguna otra condicionante para los arquitectos, que plantean con esta intervención un paseo arquitectónico a través de las estancias de la vivienda. Para lograrlo, la casa se vació hasta sus cimientos y se introdujo un eje

☐ Die Architekten beschreiben dieses Gebäude als zwei Hälften, die unabhängig voneinander funktionierten, und aus denen man eine einzige, weite und helle Wohnung gemacht hat. Außer der Tatsache, dass es zwei Schlafzimmer geben musste, gab es keine andere Vorgabe für die Architekten, die diesen Eingriff in Form eines architektonischen Spaziergangs durch die Räume des Hauses angingen. Dazu wurde das Haus ganz geleert

longitudinal en la parte superior que articula los diferentes espacios de la vivienda. Una galería de doble altura vincula las dos plantas de la casa, que antes se encontraban completamente aisladas. En esta galería se introduce una fina escalera metálica que se percibe como elemento escultórico y al mismo tiempo divisorio entre el salón y la biblioteca. Pocos materiales y colores, separados unos de otros, acompañan esta idea de espacio. El pavimento de la planta baja, de uso más público, es de piedra arenisca, mientras que en la planta superior, en donde se ubican las zonas más privadas, el suelo está definido por parqué de madera. El color beige de las paredes, a medio camino entre el color de la piedra y el de la madera, crea un efecto monolítico de gran tranquilidad.

und eine Längsachse im oberen Teil eingeführt, an der entlang sich die verschiedenen Räume gliedern. Eine Galerie in doppelter Höhe verbindet die beiden Stockwerke, die vorher absolut unabhängig voneinander waren, miteinander. Auf dieser Galerie befindet sich eine feine Metalltreppe, die wie eine Skulptur wahrgenommen wird und gleichzeitig das Wohnzimmer von der Bibliothek trennt. Diese Raumidee wird von wenig Farben, die voneinander getrennt sind, begleitet. Der Boden des Erdgeschosses, das auch von Besuchern benutzt wird, ist aus Sandstein, während der Boden des Obergeschosses, in dem sich die Privaträume befinden, mit Holzparkett belegt ist. Die Wände sind beige, die Farbe vermittelt zwischen der des Steines und der des Holzes. So entsteht eine sehr einheitlich wirkende und somit beruhigende Wirkung.

› **Ground floor**
› Planta baja
› Erdegeschoss

› **First floor**
› Planta primera
› Erster Stock

› **Second floor**
› Planta segunda
› Zweiter Stock

0 2 4

› Elevations
› Alzados
› Aufrisse

› Sections
› Secciones
› Schnitte

1. What historical reference in particular inspires you when designing a residence?

   ¿Qué referente histórico en particular le sirve de fuente de inspiración a la hora de proyectar una vivienda?

   Welche historische Referenz dient Ihnen als Inspiration beim Entwurf eines Hauses?

2. What is the main factor taken into consideration when designing a residence?

   ¿Cuál es el principal factor determinante a la hora de diseñar una vivienda?

   Welche Rahmenbedingungen, bzw. Faktoren sind für Sie ausschlaggebend beim Konzipieren?

3. What room inside the home do you find most interesting to design?

   ¿Qué estancia de la vivienda encuentra usted más interesante para diseñar?

   Welchen Raum des Hauses finden Sie am spannendsten zu entwerfen?

4. What is your criteria for choosing materials and finishings in a particular room?

   ¿Cuál es su criterio a la hora de seleccionar los materiales y los acabados en esta estancia?

   Welche Kriterien wenden Sie bei der Entscheidung über Materialen und Oberflächen in diesem Raum an?

---

1. Perhaps it is the buildings that were constructed over generations without a particular plan. Houses that have been subject to changes, adaptations, and additions in response to the needs of their occupants. I find the pursuit of modernization, where form rigorously follows function, to be an overly confining, almost boring approach.

2. The location. The building can make the place and the place can make the building; I am interested in this type of dialogue.

3. Every connecting space in a house. The rooms that can survive without having a specific function designated by the contractor.

4. The most interesting secondary rooms are those that do not have to conform to any particular function or material. The unique characteristics of each room, together with a certain atmosphere, develop during the creative process.

---

1. Son quizás aquellas construcciones que desde varias generaciones se han levantando sin un plan general. Casas que han sufrido modificaciones, adaptaciones y ampliaciones en relación tanto con sus inquilinos como con su uso. La consecución de la modernidad, donde la forma ha de seguir rigurosamente la función, me parece demasiado encorsetado, casi aburrido.

2. El lugar. A mí me interesa esa dialéctica que un edificio puede hacer al lugar, así como el lugar hace al edificio.

3. Todos los espacios conectores de una casa. Son aquellas habitaciones de la vivienda que consiguen sobrevivir sin una función concreta frente al programa de ordenación del espacio del constructor.

4. Las estancias secundarias más interesantes son aquellas en las que no se ha de desarrollar un concepto de material único. A lo largo del proceso de creación van surgiendo las características específicas de cada habitación junto con una atmósfera determinada.

---

1. Vielleicht sind es diejenigen Bauwerke, welche ohne ersichtlichen Gesamtplan über mehrere Generationen entstanden sind. Häuser, welche sowohl bezüglich Nutzer wie auch bezüglich Nutzung Änderungen, Anpassungen und Erweiterungen erfahren haben. Die Forderung der Moderne, wo Form strikte der Funktion zu folgen hat, scheint mir zu einengend, gar langweilig. Alles bleibt ablesbar und voraussehbar.

2. Der ORT. Mich interessiert diese Dialektik, dass ein Gebäude den Ort machen kann sowie eben auch der Ort das Gebäude macht.

3. Alle Zwischenräume eines Hauses. Es sind dies diejenigen Räume des Hauses, welche es gegenüber dem Raumprogramm des Bauherrn schaffen, ohne bestimmte Nutzungszuordnung zu überleben.

4. Die spannendsten Raumfolgen sind diejenigen, bei welchen nicht ein einheitliches Materialkonzept durchgezogen werden muss. Im Verlauf des Entwurfsprozesses schälen sich für die jeweiligen Räume spezifische Eigenschaften und schliesslich eine Atmosphäre heraus.

Leo Frei, founder of Frei Architekten, was born in Zurich in 1958, where he also pursued his architecture studies. After earning his degree in 1983 he added a Master of Architecture degree from the Technological Institute in Atlanta. After working in different architectural firms for several years he started his own office in 1991, in Zurich and Stäfa. He complements his work as an architect with academic duties as a professor, assistant, and instructor in various Swiss universities.

Leo Frei, fundador de Frei Architekten, nació en 1958 en Zurich, ciudad en donde adquirió sus estudios de arquitectura. Después de obtener su título en 1983, complementó sus estudios con un máster en Arquitectura en el Instituto Tecnológico de Atlanta. Tras colaborar durante varios años en diferentes despachos de arquitectura, fundó su propia oficina en 1991, en Zurich y Stäfa. Su trabajo como arquitecto lo complementa con su actividad docente como profesor, asistente y tutor en varias universidades suizas.

Leo Frei, der Gründer von Frei Architekten, kam 1958 in Zürich auf die Welt, wo er auch Architektur studierte. Nach Abschluss seines Diploms im Jahr 1983 erwarb er noch einen Master am Technological Institute in Atlanta. Nachdem er mehrere Jahre lang in verschiedenen Architekturbüros mitgearbeitet hatte, gründete er 1991 sein eigenes Unternehmen in Zürich und Stäfa. Seine Arbeit als Architekt ergänzt er mit seiner Lehrtätigkeit als Professor, Assistent und Tutor an verschiedenen Universitäten in der Schweiz.

☐ For this project the client wanted to create a private residence by combining two typical commercial mews in London. This was a complicated task due to the difficult conditions on both the exterior and interior of the original structures. The first challenge was to obtain permission from the local authorities to change the property's zoning from commercial to residential. The restrictions of the façade and the lack of any space around the property called for a strategy that consisted of opening up the rear of the building as much as possible and creating light and subtle barriers inside. This approach created a space that was open, ventilated, and well lit. Several skylights as well as the placement of a few interior mirrors brighten the space and make it feel even more open. The remodeling also created a cohesive composition from the previous series of subdivided spaces, which were different in character from each other. Most of the interior walls were removed and a common language was created based on the consistent use of materials and finishes throughout the two units. The rich color and texture of the materials create a soft, warm atmosphere that is more appropriate for the new residential function.

London Mews Conversion

› co-labarchitects

London, UK › 2003 › Photos © Mat Jessop

☐ El cliente de este proyecto quería crear una residencia privada con la unión de dos típicas vías comerciales de Londres. Una tarea complicada debido a las difíciles condiciones de las estructuras originales tanto del exterior como del interior. El primer reto fue obtener el permiso de las autoridades locales para cambiar el uso de la propiedad comercial en residencial. Las restricciones de la fachada y la ausencia de espacio exterior en la propiedad

☐ Der Kunde gab eine Privatwohnung in Auftrag, für die zwei kommerziell genutzte Mews (ehemalige umgebaute Stallungen) in London vereint und renoviert werden sollten. Das war aufgrund der schwierigen, äußeren und inneren Struktur der Originalgebäude eine komplizierte Aufgabe. Zunächst musste man überhaupt eine Baugenehmigung bekommen, um aus einem Geschäftsgebäude ein Wohnhaus machen zu dürfen. An

requirieron una estrategia basada en abrir al máximo la parte posterior del espacio y crear barreras interiores ambiguas y ligeras. Con esto se consiguió lograr un espacio abierto, ventilado y diáfano. Una serie de lucernarios así como la disposición de algunos espejos interiores, contribuyen a iluminar el espacio y percibirlo aún más abierto. El proyecto también creó una composición cohesiva de lo que antes era una serie de espacios subdivididos y con diferente carácter entre sí. Esto se logró cambiando la mayoría de las paredes interiores y creando un mismo lenguaje a partir de los materiales y los acabados en las dos unidades. Los materiales, ricos en textura y color, crean atmósferas suaves y cálidas, más apropiadas para el nuevo uso residencial.

der Fassade durfte nicht viel geändert werden und außen gab es keinen Platz, deshalb musste der Raum so weit wie möglich nach hinten geöffnet werden, und die inneren Abtrennungen sollten mehrdeutig und leicht sein. So entstanden offene, luftige und helle Räume. Durch verschiedene Dachfenster und Spiegel im Inneren wird das Licht verteilt und der Eindruck von offenen Räumen noch verstärkt. Außerdem wurde Nachdruck auf eine zusammenhängende Komposition der Räume gelegt, die vorher unterteilt und sehr verschieden waren. Das erreichte man durch den Abriss der meisten Innenwände und den Einsatz von ähnlichen Materialien und Stilen in beiden Einheiten. Die Materialien mit ihrer reichen Textur und Farbigkeit schaffen eine sanfte und warme, wohnliche Atmosphäre in den neuen Räumen.

0 2 4

› **Ground floor**

› Planta baja

› Erdegeschoss

› **First floor**

› Planta primera

› Erster Stock

› **Sections**

› Secciones

› Schnitte

› **Elevations**

› Alzados

› Aufrisse

› Details

› Detalles

› Details

1. What historical reference in particular inspires you when designing a residence?

¿Qué referente histórico en particular le sirve de fuente de inspiración a la hora de proyectar una vivienda?

Welche historische Referenz dient Ihnen als Inspiration beim Entwurf eines Hauses?

2. What is the main factor taken into consideration when designing a residence?

¿Cuál es el principal factor determinante a la hora de diseñar una vivienda?

Welche Rahmenbedingungen, bzw. Faktoren sind für Sie ausschlaggebend beim Konzipieren?

3. What room inside the home do you find most interesting to design?

¿Qué estancia de la vivienda encuentra usted más interesante para diseñar?

Welchen Raum des Hauses finden Sie am spannendsten zu entwerfen?

4. What is your criteria for choosing materials and finishings in a particular room?

¿Cuál es su criterio a la hora de seleccionar los materiales y los acabados en esta estancia?

Welche Kriterien wenden Sie bei der Entscheidung über Materialen und Oberflächen in diesem Raum an?

1. The house of John Soane in London was designed to house his large collection of art and antiquities. The plasticity and ambiguity of the spaces and the manipulation of natural daylight raises the architecture to a spiritual level.

2. The aspirations of the client is the most important aspect of designing a residence. The goal of the designer is to exceed these aspirations and realize space beyond the client's own imagination.

3. The living space is the social hub of all houses and it's relationship to the other spaces is critical. The definition of this space is all encompassing, it can sometimes be the only room in a studio apartment.

4. We are moving away from white minimalist space by using colour and texture more and more in our projects.

1. La casa de John Sloan en Londres fue diseñada para albergar su gran colección de arte y antigüedades. La plasticidad y ambigüedad de los espacios y la manipulación de la luz natural elevan la arquitectura a un grado espiritual.

2. Las expectativas del cliente son el aspecto más importante al diseñar una vivienda. El objetivo del diseñador es sobrepasar esas expectativas y crear un espacio más allá de la imaginación del cliente.

3. El espacio público es el centro social de todas las viviendas y su relación con el resto de espacio es muy importante. La definición de este espacio lo engloba todo; a veces puede ser la única habitación en un apartamento.

4. Nos estamos alejando de los blancos espacios minimalistas al incluir cada vez más el color y la textura en nuestros diseños.

1. Das Haus von John Sloan in London wurde entworfen, um seine große Kunst- und Antiquitätensammlung aufzunehmen. Die Plastizität und Zweideutigkeit der Räume und der Umgang mit dem Tageslicht erhöhen die Architektur auf eine spirituelle Ebene.

2. Die Wünsche des Kunden sind der wichtigste Aspekt beim Entwurf einer Wohnung oder eines Wohnhauses. Ziel des Gestalters ist es, diese Erwartungen noch zu übertreffen und einen Raum zu schaffen, der noch über die Vorstellungskraft des Auftraggebers hinaus geht.

3. Der von allen genutzte Raum ist der soziale Mittelpunkt aller Wohnungen und seine Beziehung zu den übrigen Räumen ist sehr wichtig. Die Definition dieses Raumes bezieht alles mit ein. Manchmal kann es sich dabei um den einzigen Raum in einem Appartement handeln.

4. Wir entfernen uns allmählich von den weißen, minimalistischen Räumen, um im stärkeren Maße wieder Farbe und Textur in unsere Entwürfe einzuführen.

The founders of co-labarchitects have worked for many design firms, on both small and large-scale projects, as design architects and design group leaders before establishing co-labarchitects in 2001. Their design approach focuses on responding positively to the client and to the project's environment in order to materialize the aspirations and potential of each. Co-labarchitects feel that it is important to adapt the needs of the client and at the same time take full advantage of the natural characteristics of each location, finding inspiration from various sources to create proposals based on logical analysis.

Los fundadores de co-labarchitects han trabajado para muchas firmas de diseño, en proyectos de gran y pequeña escala, en calidad de arquitectos diseñadores y jefes de grupo de diseño hasta establecer la firma en 2001. Su enfoque de diseño es el de responder positivamente al cliente y al entorno del proyecto con el objetivo de materializar las aspiraciones y las potencialidades de cada uno. Co-labarchitects considera importante adaptar las necesidades del cliente, y al mismo tiempo explotar las naturaleza de cada lugar, tomando varias fuentes de inspiración para crear propuestas basadas en un análisis lógico.

Die Gründer von co-labarchitects haben bereits für viele Unternehmen im Bereich Innenarchitektur gearbeitet, sowohl in großen als auch in kleinen Projekten. Im Jahre 2001 gründeten sie co-labarchitects. Mit ihren Entwürfen möchten sie die Anforderungen des jeweiligen Kunden und der Umgebung jedes Gebäudes gerecht werden. Für co-labarchitects ist es wichtig, die Bedürfnisse des Kunden zu verstehen und gleichzeitig den Charakter des jeweiligen Ortes als Inspirationsquelle zu nutzen, die man analysiert und als Grundlage der Planung benutzt.

☐ This loft, located in the Flatiron District in the center of New York, was remodeled by the same architect once before in 1990, when it was adapted as a residence and photographic studio. Now with a new family, the client requested another total renovation, this time to turn the entire space into an apartment. The auxiliary spaces like bedrooms, bathrooms, and the television room are laid out around the "great room", which includes the living, dining, and play areas. The kitchen, fully equipped with the latest technology, is at one side of this space. Since most of the windows are located only on the south side of the residence, bright colors and glossy finishes were used to help reflect the natural light in the interior. A glass brick wall that separates the kitchen from a public hallway in the building allows light to flow into the apartment, and it becomes a large-scale lamp at night. The materials and finishes used for the interior, like mosaic tiles, maple wood, and natural stone, were chosen for their minimal maintenance requirements.

Flatiron District Loft

› Donald Billinkoff Architects

New York, NY, USA › 2003 › Photos © Elliott Kaufman Photography

☐ Este loft, ubicado en el céntrico distrito de Flatiron de Nueva York, fue remodelado por primera vez por el mismo arquitecto en 1990 para adaptarlo como estudio de fotografía y residencia. Con una nueva familia, el cliente pidió de nuevo una reforma integral, en este caso para destinar la superficie total del espacio como vivienda. Los espacios auxiliares como habitaciones, baños y el cuarto de la televisión están organizados en torno a una

☐ Dieses Loft im zentral gelegenen Flatiron District in New York wurde 1990 zum ersten Mal von dem Architekten selbst zu einem Fotografiestudio und Wohnung umgebaut. Aufgrund seiner neuen Familie gab der Kunde eine neue Gesamtrenovierung in Auftrag, um sämtliche Räume zu Wohnräumen umzugestalten. Die Nebenräume wie Schlafzimmer, Bäder und der Fernsehraum sind um das "große Zimmer" herum ange-

gran área que incluye la zona de estar, el comedor y un espacio para juegos. La cocina, equipada con la última tecnología, está junto a esta área. Ya que la mayoría de las ventanas están ubicadas solamente en la parte sur de la vivienda, se optó por utilizar colores y acabados brillantes que contribuyeran a reflejar la luz natural en el interior. Una pared de bloques de vidrio, que divide la cocina de un corredor público del edificio, permite el paso de la luz al interior y durante la noche funciona como una lámpara de gran formato. Los materiales y los acabados interiores, como el mosaico, la madera de arce o la piedra natural, fueron elegidos pensando en su fácil mantenimiento.

ordnet, in dem sich Wohn-, Ess- und Spielzimmer befindet. Die vollständig mit modernster Technologie ausgestattete Küche liegt neben diesem Raum. Da die meisten Fenster der Wohnung nach Süden liegen, wurden glänzende Farben und Oberflächen gewählt, die das Tageslicht im Inneren widerspiegeln. Eine Wand aus Glasbausteinen trennt die Küche von dem Flur, den alle Gebäudebewohner benutzen. Sie lässt Tageslicht einfallen und wirkt nachts wie eine riesige Lampe. Die im Inneren verwendeten Materialien wie Mosaiken, Ahornholz und Naturstein wurden ausgewählt, weil sie so pflegeleicht sind.

0   2   4

› **Previous plan**

› Planta original

› Originalgrundriss

› **New plan**

› Planta nueva

› Never Grundriss

0 2 4

> Sections
> Secciones
> Schnitte

1. What historical reference in particular inspires you when designing a residence?
   ¿Qué referente histórico en particular le sirve de fuente de inspiración a la hora de proyectar una vivienda?
   Welche historische Referenz dient Ihnen als Inspiration beim Entwurf eines Hauses?

2. What is the main factor taken into consideration when designing a residence?
   ¿Cuál es el principal factor determinante a la hora de diseñar una vivienda?
   Welche Rahmenbedingungen, bzw. Faktoren sind für Sie ausschlaggebend beim Konzipieren?

3. What room inside the home do you find most interesting to design?
   ¿Qué estancia de la vivienda encuentra usted más interesante para diseñar?
   Welchen Raum des Hauses finden Sie am spannendsten zu entwerfen?

4. What is your criteria for choosing materials and finishings in a particular room?
   ¿Cuál es su criterio a la hora de seleccionar los materiales y los acabados en esta estancia?
   Welche Kriterien wenden Sie bei der Entscheidung über Materialen und Oberflächen in diesem Raum an?

1. Our goal is appropriateness: for the site, for the client, for the budget. Of course, our primary interest is contemporary architecture, but we often use evocative materials and colors if they are appropriate.

2. We begin the design process by looking at the site, primarily access and lnatural light. With an idea of how best to use the site we then look at the functional organization of the home: flow, adjacencies, program, etc. As the plan begins to develop we start our investigation of the massing and building form.

3. I can't say there is one particular room we find more interesting than others.

4. Our preference is for contemporary design; simple detailing. But we also prefer that our homes be warm and habitable.

1. Nuestro objetivo es la corrección: para el lugar, para el cliente, para el presupuesto. Nuestro interés primordial es la arquitectura contemporánea, claro está, pero a menudo utilizamos materiales y colores evocadores si son apropiados.

2. Empezamos el proceso de diseño observando el solar, principalmente su acceso y la luz que recibe. Con la idea de cómo aprovechar el lugar al máximo, comenzamos a pensar en la organización funcional de la vivienda: la distribución, el programa, etcétera; a medida que se desarrolla el plano, investigamos sobre la forma estructural del edificio.

3. No hay una habitación que nos parezca más interesante que otra.

4. Nuestra preferencia es el diseño moderno, los detalles sencillos, pero nos gusta que nuestras viviendas sean cálidas y habitables.

1. Unser Ziel ist es, dass alles stimmt, für den Standort, für den Kunden, für das Budget. Unser Hauptinteresse gilt der zeitgenössischen Architektur, aber natürlich benutzen wir auch manchmal Materialien und Farben, die auf andere Epochen anspielen, wenn es in den Kontext passt.

2. Wir beginnen die Planung eines Bauvorhabens mit einer Studie des Grundstücks, wobei wir hauptsächlich den Zugang und die Lichtverhältnisse betrachten. So entsteht zunächst eine Idee, wie man den Ort maximal ausnutzen kann. Dann beginnen wir, an die funktionelle Organisation des Wohnhauses zu denken, die Verteilung, die Wohnfunktionen usw.. In dem Maße, in dem der Plan weiter entwickelt wird, fangen wir an, uns über die Form des Gebäudes Gedanken zu machen.

3. Es gibt keinen Raum, den wir interessanter als die übrigen Räume finden.

4. Wir bevorzugen modernes Design mit einfachen Einzelheiten, aber wir möchten warme und wohnliche Räume schaffen.

Donald Billinkoff Architects is an architecture and interior design firm based in New York and founded in 1992. It specializes in the design of residential, commercial, and institutional projects in the New York, New Jersey, Connecticut, and Pennsylvania areas. Their projects, the new construction as well as the renovations, have been featured in many international magazines.

Donald Billinkoff Architects es una firma de arquitectura y diseño interior, con sede en Nueva York y fundada en 1992. Se dedica al diseño de proyectos residenciales, comerciales e institucionales en las zonas de Nueva York, Nueva Jersey, Connecticut y Pensilvania. Se ha destacado su trabajo, dedicado tanto a la obra nueva como a las renovaciones, en numerosas publicaciones internacionales.

Donald Billinkoff Architects ist ein Büro für Architektur und Innenarchitektur in New York, das 1992 gegründet wurde. Hauptsächlich werden hier Wohn- und Geschäftshäuser und Gebäude für Institutionen in den Regionen New York, New Jersey, Connecticut und Pennsylvania geplant. Sowohl die Neu- als auch die Umbauten dieses Architekten wurden in zahlreichen, internationalen Zeitschriften vorgestellt.

☐ This loft is located on the twelfth floor of a commercial building in New York's Soho neighborhood, and it functions as a permanent design laboratory where materials, models, and prototypes are incorporated into the construction details of the loft. A great variety of materials are used to stimulate the senses, and the various rooms are easily accessible, much like the quarters in a sailboat. The flexibility of the interior is primarily achieved with the furniture, which was especially designed by the architect herself. The flexibility of the furniture and the many ways it can be arranged allow the space to be used as a residence, architectural office, exhibit space, or for entertaining. The space is organized into three main bodies: a central one used as a living room or exhibit space; another one where the kitchen and the meeting space is located; and finally, the bedroom or most private studio. The larger than normal doors, including one in the kitchen that is made of glass, encourage the integration between the different areas.

Flexible Loft

› Page Goolrick Architect

New York, NY, USA › 2000 › Photos © John M. Hall

☐ Este loft se encuentra ubicado en la duodécima planta de un edificio comercial del Soho, en Nueva York, y funciona como un laboratorio permanente de diseño en donde los materiales, los modelos y los prototipos se incorporan en los detalles de la construcción del loft. Se emplea una gran variedad de materiales con el objeto de crear estímulos para los sentidos y las diferentes habitaciones del interior son de fácil accesibilidad, como si se

☐ Dieses Loft befindet sich im zwölften Stockwerk eines Geschäftshauses in Soho in New York. Es stellt eine Art permanentes Labor für Design dar, in dem Materialien, Modelle und Prototypen sich in die Konstruktionselemente des Lofts selbst einfügen. Man verwendete eine Vielzahl von Materialien, um die Sinne anzuregen. Gleichzeitig sind alle Zimmer im Inneren leicht zu erreichen, so als ob man sich in einem Segelschiff befände.

tratara del interior de un velero. La flexibilidad del interior se logra principalmente por medio del mobiliario que fue especialmente diseñado por la misma arquitecta. La movilidad de los muebles así como las diversas posibilidades de configuración permite aprovechar el espacio, ya sea como vivienda, oficina de arquitectura, sala de exhibición o de entretenimiento. El espacio está organizado en tres cuerpos principales: uno central, o exhibición, que se utiliza como sala de estar; otro en el que se ubica la cocina y al mismo tiempo la sala de reuniones, y la habitación o estudio más privado. Las puertas de gran formato, y de cristal en el caso de la cocina, permiten una mayor integración entre los diferentes espacios.

Die Flexibilität des Inneren wird hauptsächlich durch die Möbel erreicht, die vom gleichen Architekten entworfen wurden. Die Beweglichkeit der Möbel und die verschiedenen Gestaltungsmöglichkeiten lassen es zu, dass dieser Raum als Wohnung, Architekturbüro, Ausstellungssaal oder Übungsraum benutzt werden kann. Der Raum ist in drei Hauptbereiche unterteilt, ein Zentralteil, der als Wohnzimmer oder Ausstellungsraum dient, ein weiterer Bereich, in dem sich die Küche, die gleichzeitig der Konferenzsaal ist, befindet, und ein Zimmer, das als privates Studio dient. Die großen Türen und die gläserne Küchentür ermöglichen die bessere Integration der verschiedenen Räumlichkeiten.

Plan

Planta

Grundriss

1. What historical reference in particular inspires you when designing a residence?
¿Qué referente histórico en particular le sirve de fuente de inspiración a la hora de proyectar una vivienda?
Welche historische Referenz dient Ihnen als Inspiration beim Entwurf eines Hauses?

2. What is the main factor taken into consideration when designing a residence?
¿Cuál es el principal factor determinante a la hora de diseñar una vivienda?
Welche Rahmenbedingungen, bzw. Faktoren sind für Sie ausschlaggebend beim Konzipieren?

3. What room inside the home do you find most interesting to design?
¿Qué estancia de la vivienda encuentra usted más interesante para diseñar?
Welchen Raum des Hauses finden Sie am spannendsten zu entwerfen?

4. What is your criteria for choosing materials and finishings in a particular room?
¿Cuál es su criterio a la hora de seleccionar los materiales y los acabados en esta estancia?
Welche Kriterien wenden Sie bei der Entscheidung über Materialen und Oberflächen in diesem Raum an?

1. Case study houses of the forties and fifties as they had open plans, an emphasis on natural light, efficient use of space and the economical use of simple materials.

2. The site, light, views, and natural ventilation are celebrated and maximized whether we are working on an urban loft or a freestanding structure in a rural context.

3. The hub, or the most heavily used space where the family comes together and where they socialize with others. The hub may be the living room, a family room or what is often referred to as the great room where all the social activities overlap.

4. Functionality, beauty, easy of maintenance, texture, durability and we like to introduce clients to materials they may be familiar with used in a new way.

1. Las casas típicas de la década de 1940 y 1950 con sus plantas abiertas, el énfasis en la luz natural, el uso eficiente del espacio y la economía en el empleo de los materiales.

2. El lugar, la luz, las vistas y la ventilación natural siempre son destacados en cualquier tipo de proyecto en el que trabajamos, desde un loft urbano hasta una estructura aislada en un entorno rural.

3. El punto neurálgico o el espacio más utilizado donde la familia se suele reunir y se relaciona. Este punto puede ser la sala de estar, una sala familiar o lo que algunas veces se refiere a una gran habitación en donde todas las actividades sociales se integran.

4. Funcionalidad, belleza, fácil mantenimiento, textura, durabilidad y el deseo de mostrar a los clientes una nueva manera de utilizar los materiales.

1. Die typischen Häuser aus den Vierziger und Fünfzigerjahren mit ihren offenen Stockwerken, die Bedeutung des Tageslicht, die effiziente Nutzung der Räume und die Sparsamkeit beim Einsatz von Materilien.

2. Der Standort, das Licht, die Aussicht und die natürliche Lüftung sind in jedem unserer Bauvorhaben wichtig. Das gilt sowohl für die Fabriketage in der Stadt als auch für ein einzeln stehendes Gebäude in einer ländlichen Umgebung.

3. Das Zentrum oder der meistbenutzte Raum, in dem sich die Familie trifft oder in dem sie Gäste empfängt. Dieser Ort kann das Wohnzimmer sein, ein Familienzimmer oder manchmal ein großer Raum, in dem sich alle sozialen Aktivitäten überschneiden.

4. Funktionalität, Schönheit, einfache Pflege, Textur, Haltbarkeit und der Wunsch, den Kunden einen neuen Umgang mit den Materialien zu zeigen.

Page Goolrick Architect is an architecture and interior design firm based in New York since 1988. The firm's team operates under the shared belief that design excellence results from a simple, clear, and rational attitude, which will create structures that are suitable for our own time period as well as for each specific context and project. The firm's goal is to be able to simplify everyday functions, and in that way fulfill the varied interests and spatial requirements of each client.

Page Goolrick Architect es una firma de arquitectura y diseño interior con sede en Nueva York desde 1988. El equipo que compone la firma opera en la creencia compartida de que la excelencia en el diseño se logra por medio de una actitud sencilla, clara y racional para crear estructuras adecuadas tanto para nuestro tiempo como para cada programa y contexto específico. El objetivo de la firma es lograr simplificar las funciones diarias y de este modo celebrar la variedad de intereses y las necesidades espaciales de cada cliente.

Page Goolrick Architect ist ein Architekturbüro, das seit 1988 in New York tätig ist. Dieses Architektenteam folgt der Devise, dass man ein ausgezeichnetes Design durch eine einfache, klare und rationale Haltung erreicht, um so Strukturen zu schaffen, die für unsere spezifische Zeit geeignet sind, und zwar für jeden Zweck und Kontext. Ziel des Büros ist es, die täglichen Funktionen zu vereinfachen und so den verschiedenen Interessen jedes Kunden gerecht zu werden und Räume für alle Bedürfnisse zu schaffen.

☐ The Sempacher building, located in a desirable residential area of Zurich, is an excellent example of modern and sustainable urban restoration. The lot was occupied by a monotonous apartment block from the 1930's that urgently needed to be brought up to date. A detailed preliminary study showed that everything from the electrical installations to the plumbing needed to be upgraded, but that the structure itself would not permit any improvements in the quality of the spaces. A decision was made to replace the building with a new one that would incorporate three main characteristics: a flexible structure that would allow future generations to make changes; a modern building that would maintain a harmonious dialogue with the surrounding structures; and a structure that was sensitive to its environment, taking into account the life cycles of its materials. The spaces have a utility core where the kitchens and bathrooms are located, allowing the living quarters to be more flexible. The building is covered with overlapping translucent pieces that protect it from the sun. Both the color and the texture created by this shell help the building fit into its urban surroundings.

Sempacher Apartments

› Camenzind Evolution

Zurich, Switzerland › 2002 › Photos © Camenzind Evolution

☐ Ubicados en una privilegiada zona residencial de Zurich, los apartamentos Sempacher son un excelente ejemplo de renovación urbana moderna y sostenible. El solar estaba ocupado por un monótono bloque de apartamentos de 1930 que necesitaba una adecuación urgente. Un estudio previo detallado demostró que todo el conjunto, desde la instalación eléctrica hasta la de tuberías, necesitaban una actualización, teniendo en cuenta que la estructura

☐ Das Sempacher-Haus, das in einer gepflegten Wohngegend in Zürich liegt, ist ein ausgezeichnetes Beispiel für die moderne und umweltfreundliche Restaurierung eines Stadtgebäudes. Auf dem Grundstück befand sich ein eintöniger, renovierungsbedürftiger Wohnblock aus den Dreißigerjahren. Die vorherige Gebäudeanalyse ergab, dass das gesamte Gebäude einschließlich elektrischer und sanitärer Installationen

no permitía mejoras en cuanto a la calidad de los espacios. Se decidió reemplazar el edificio por uno nuevo que cumpliera principalmente tres características: una estructura flexible y que permitiera cambios para las futuras generaciones; un edificio moderno que dialogara armónicamente con su entorno construido, y una construcción sensible con el medio ambiente prestando atención en los ciclos de vida de los materiales. Se dispuso un centro de servicios, en el cual se ubican las cocinas y los baños, y así las áreas de estar cuentan con más flexibilidad. El edificio está revestido de piezas translúcidas sobrepuestas que protegen de la incidencia del sol. Tanto el color como la textura lograda por este revestimiento contribuyen a que el edificio se integre en el entorno urbano en el que se encuentra.

modernisierst werden musste, dass aber die Struktur selbst keine Verbesserung der Qualität der Räume zuließ. So entschied man sich für einen Abriss und einen Neubau, der folgende Eigenschaften haben sollte: eine flexible Struktur, die Veränderungen für künftige Generationen erlaubt, ein modernes Gebäude, das sich harmonisch in die Umgebung einfügt und eine umweltgerechte Bauweise unter Berücksichtigung der Lebensdauer der Materialien. Küchen und Bäder befinden sich alle im gleichen Bereich, so dass die Wohnräume flexibler gestaltet werden konnten. Das Gebäude besitzt eine lichtdurchlässige, sich überlappende Verkleidung, die vor direkter Sonne schützt. Sowohl die Farbe als auch die Textur dieser Verkleidung tragen dazu bei, dass sich das Gebäude perfekt in seine Umgebung einfügt.

› **Ground floor**

› Planta baja

› Erdgeschoss

0 3 6

› **First floor**

› Planta primera

› Erster Stock

› **Second floor**

› Planta segunda

› Zweiter Stock

› **Sections**

› Secciones

› Schnitte

› **Elevations**

› Alzados

› Aufrisse

1. What historical reference in particular inspires you when designing a residence?

¿Qué referente histórico en particular le sirve de fuente de inspiración a la hora de proyectar una vivienda?

Welche historische Referenz dient Ihnen als Inspiration beim Entwurf eines Hauses?

2. What is the main factor taken into consideration when designing a residence?

¿Cuál es el principal factor determinante a la hora de diseñar una vivienda?

Welche Rahmenbedingungen, bzw. Faktoren sind für Sie ausschlaggebend beim Konzipieren?

3. What room inside the home do you find most interesting to design?

¿Qué estancia de la vivienda encuentra usted más interesante para diseñar?

Welchen Raum des Hauses finden Sie am spannendsten zu entwerfen?

4. What is your criteria for choosing materials and finishings in a particular room?

¿Cuál es su criterio a la hora de seleccionar los materiales y los acabados en esta estancia?

Welche Kriterien wenden Sie bei der Entscheidung über Materialen und Oberflächen in diesem Raum an?

1. Our experiences have taught us the importance of local events and microstructures. Especially important to our work is the respect of people's local identity and roots.

2. Architecture is in most cases not the staging of the special, but the design of the common. Like our clothes, buildings must not only fulfil practical, but also emotional requirements. We are not interested in designing just technically perfect buildings that have no 'emotional responders' and therefore feel cold and dead to the user.

3. It's never one room but always the movement between rooms, which creates the space and the emotional experience within it.

4. Materials, finishes and colour are some of the many ingredients of architecture. But we see these ingredients more as an 'enhancer' of conceptions or emotional intentions.

1. Nuestras experiencias nos han enseñado la importancia de las circunstancias concretas y las microestructuras. La identidad de las personas y sus raíces son especialmente importantes en nuestro trabajo.

2. La arquitectura no es, en la mayoría de los casos, el escenario de lo especial, sino el diseño de lo común. Como nuestra ropa, los edificios no sólo deben cumplir requisitos prácticos, sino también emocionales. No estamos interesados en diseñar edificios técnicamente perfectos que no provocan respuestas emocionales y resultan fríos para el habitante.

3. No se trata de una habitación, sino la movilidad entre ellas, que crea un espacio y la experiencia emocional en ellas.

4. Los materiales, los acabados y la gama cromática son algunos de los muchos ingredientes de la arquitectura, pero son elementos que refuerzan los conceptos, no las intenciones emocionales.

1. Unsere Erfahrungen haben uns die Bedeutung punktueller Umstände und von Mikrostrukturen gelehrt. Die Identität von Personen und ihre Wurzeln sind besonders wichtig für unsere Arbeit.

2. Die Architektur ist in den meisten Fällen nicht der Schauplatz des Besonderen, sondern die Gestaltung des Gewöhnlichen. Wie unsere Kleidung sollten auch Gebäude nicht nur praktische Anforderungen erfüllen, sondern auch emotionale. Es interessiert uns nicht, technisch perfekte Gebäude zu entwerfen, die keine Gefühle wach rufen und auf den Benutzer kalt wirken.

3. Es ist nicht ein Raum, sondern die Bewegung zwischen den Räumen, was den Raum und die emotionale Erfahrung innerhalb des Raumes schafft.

4. Die Materialien, Oberflächen und Farben sind nur einige der vielen Zutaten der Architektur, aber sie sind die Elemente, die die emotionalen Konzepte oder Absichten verstärken.

Architects Stefan Camenzind and Michael Grafensteiner, winners of the Young Architect of the Year Award and the International Design Prize, have firmly positioned themselves among the new generation of notable architects. Their work stands out for its fusion of ingenuity and typical Swiss quality. Stefan Camenzind and Michael Grafensteiner founded their own studio in 1995, after having gained experience working in architectural offices in London, Paris, and Los Angeles. At present they have more than 15 architects practicing with them.

Ganadores del premio Joven Arquitecto del Año y el premio de Diseño Internacional, los arquitectos Stefan Camenzind y Michael Grafensteiner forman parte de la nueva generación de arquitectos notables. Su trabajo está influenciado fundamentalmente por una fusión de ingenuidad y calidad típicamente suiza. Después de tener experiencia trabajando en oficinas de arquitectura en Londres, París y Los Ángeles, Stefan Camenzind y Michael Grafensteiner fundaron su propio estudio en 1995 y en la actualidad cuentan con más de 15 arquitectos colaboradores.

Die Architekten Stefan Camenzind und Michael Grafensteiner, Preisträger des Young Architect of the Year-Preises und des International Design Award, gehören mittlerweile zur neuen Generation berühmter Architekten. Ihre Arbeit ist vor allem von der Vermischung von Naivität mit der für die Schweiz so typischen Qualität gekennzeichnet. Nachdem sie bereits für Architekturbüros in London, Paris und Los Angeles gearbeitet hatten, gründeten Stefan Camenzind und Michael Grafensteiner 1995 ihr eigenes Studio, in dem gegenwärtig 15 Architekten zusammenarbeiten.

☐ The first step in renovating this loft was to eliminate as many interior walls as possible in order to create a greater feeling of space and light. Very light and flexible materials and design elements were used to fulfill the requirements of the project while preserving the proportions of the space that had been created. The guest room, for example, consists of a foldout bed and two curtains that define the space. The close collaboration of the architects, Roger Hirsch and Miriam Corti, and the interior design team Tocar Inc., was vital in creating the clean and striking atmosphere they were striving for. Materials such as ebony wood, sheer curtains, and Peruvian ceramics created a very elegant and sophisticated atmosphere. The choice of furniture was inspired by the clientís extensive collection of art and photographs in which lively, intense colors are dominant. A palette of soft colors and earth tones was chosen, as well as a few pieces of furniture that would have great impact on the space.

Loft in Tribeca

› Roger Hirsch, Myriam Corti + Tocar Inc.

New York, NY, USA › 2002 › Photos © Michael Moran

☐ La primera operación en la reforma de este loft consistió en eliminar la mayor cantidad de paredes interiores posibles con el objeto de ganar una mayor sensación de espacio y luminosidad. Para conservar las proporciones del espacio que se consiguió descubrir, pero al mismo tiempo incorporar el programa requerido para la vivienda, se recurrió a materiales y elementos de diseño muy ligeros y flexibles. La habitación de huéspedes, por ejemplo,

☐ Der erste Schritt bei der Renovierung dieses Lofts bestand in der Beseitigung möglichst vieler Innenwände, um den Eindruck von mehr Raum und Licht zu gewinnen. Um die Proportionen des neu geschaffenen Raums zu wahren, aber gleichzeitig alle notwendigen Wohnräume zu schaffen, wurden sehr leichte und flexible Materialien und Elemente verwendet. Das Gästezimmer zum Beispiel besteht aus einem Klappbett und zwei Gardinen, die den

consiste en una cama plegable y dos cortinas que definen el espacio. La colaboración estrecha entre los arquitectos, Roger Hirsch y Myriam Corti, y el equipo de interiorismo Tocar, Inc. fue vital para lograr la atmósfera clara y contundente que se buscaba. Los materiales como la madera de ébano, los vaporosos visillos o las cerámicas del Perú crean un ambiente muy cuidado y sofisticado. La elección del mobiliario estuvo inspirada en la extensa colección de arte y fotografía de los clientes en donde predominan los colores vivos e intensos. Se decidió entonces una paleta de colores suaves y tonos terrosos así como pocas piezas de mobiliario pero contundentes en el espacio.

Raum definieren. Die enge Zusammenarbeit der Architekten Roger Hirsch und Myriam Corti mit dem Innenarchitektenteam Tocar Inc trug entscheidend dazu bei, die gewünschte klare und ansprechende Atmosphäre zu schaffen. Materialien wie Ebenholz, die feinen Gardinen und Keramik aus Peru schaffen eine sehr gepflegte Atmosphäre. Die Auswahl der Möbel wurde von der umfassenden Kunst- und Fotografiesammlung der Kunden beeinflusst, in denen lebendige und intensive Farben dominieren. Deshalb wurden die Räumlichkeiten in sanften Farben und Erdtönen gestaltet, mit wenig Möbelstücken, die den Raum jedoch entscheidend gestalten.

0   1   2

› Previous plan
› Planta original
› Originalgrundriss

> New plan
> Planta nueva
> Never Grundriss

1. What historical reference in particular inspires you when designing a residence?

   ¿Qué referente histórico en particular le sirve de fuente de inspiración a la hora de proyectar una vivienda?

   Welche historische Referenz dient Ihnen als Inspiration beim Entwurf eines Hauses?

2. What is the main factor taken into consideration when designing a residence?

   ¿Cuál es el principal factor determinante a la hora de diseñar una vivienda?

   Welche Rahmenbedingungen, bzw. Faktoren sind für Sie ausschlaggebend beim Konzipieren?

3. What room inside the home do you find most interesting to design?

   ¿Qué estancia de la vivienda encuentra usted más interesante para diseñar?

   Welchen Raum des Hauses finden Sie am spannendsten zu entwerfen?

4. What is your criteria for choosing materials and finishings in a particular room?

   ¿Cuál es su criterio a la hora de seleccionar los materiales y los acabados en esta estancia?

   Welche Kriterien wenden Sie bei der Entscheidung über Materialen und Oberflächen in diesem Raum an?

---

1. We are influenced by classic modernist architects and by artists whose work inspires us.

2. The main starting points for us are the existing context, whether it be a loft interior or a wooded site for a house, and the functional needs of the clients. Our goal is to take these given perameters and then transform them into something that transcends the purely functional.

3. What is most important to us is the interconnection of rooms and how one room flows to the next. In terms of individual spaces, we like to design rooms that present specific design challenges and require inventive solutions.

4. We choose our materials based on the character of a particular room. We like to bring color and texture to surfaces through the use of natural materials.

---

1. Estamos influenciados por los clásicos arquitectos modernos y por artistas cuyo trabajo nos inspira.

2. Los puntos de partida más importantes para nosotros son el entorno, ya sea el interior de un loft o el terreno boscoso para una casa, y las necesidades funcionales de los clientes. Nuestro objetivo es tomar estos parámetros y transformarlos en algo que trascienda lo puramente funcional.

3. Lo que más nos importa es la interconexión entre las estancias y cómo una habitación fluye hacia la siguiente. En términos de espacios individuales, nos gusta diseñar habitaciones que presentan un reto de diseño concreto y requieren soluciones novedosas.

4. Escogemos los materiales según el carácter de una habitación particular. Nos gusta traer color y textura a las superficies con materiales naturales.

---

1. Wir sind von den klassischen, modernen Architekten und von Künstlern, deren Arbeit uns inspiriert, beeinflusst.

2. Die wichtigsten Ausgangspunkte für uns sind der Kontext, egal, ob es sich um das Innere einer Fabriketage oder ein Waldgrundstück für ein Haus handelt, und die funktionellen Bedürfnisse jedes Kundens. Unser Ziel ist es, diese Parameter zu erkennen und in etwas umzuformen, was das rein Funktionelle übersteigt.

3. Für uns ist die Verbindung zwischen den Räumen, und wie ein Raum zum nächsten hin fließt, am wichtigsten. Was die individuellen Räume betrifft, so genießen wir es, Räume zu gestalten, die eine besondere Herausforderung darstellen und neue Lösungen brauchen.

4. Wir wählen die Materialien entsprechend des Charakters jedes einzelnen Raumes aus. Wir bringen gerne mithilfe von natürlichen Materialien Farbe und Textur auf die Wände.

Roger Hirsch Architect (Roger Hirsch y Miryam Corti) is a design firm that specializes in residential and commercial projects. Over the past twelve years its activities have focused on specific clients and locations, resulting in innovative and functional solutions. The firm has received two awards from the Institute of American Architects (AIA) for its residential and retail store designs.

The interior design firm, Tocar, Inc., consists of Susan Vendar and Christina Sullivan. Their design proposals offer a fresh approach to the concept of elegance, mixing classic and contemporary elements.

Roger Hirsch Architect (Roger Hirsch y Miryam Corti) desarrolla proyectos residenciales y comerciales. En los últimos doce años su trabajo se ha centrado en clientes y emplazamientos concretos que dan como resultado proyectos funcionales e innovadores. La firma ha recibido dos premios del Instituto Americano de Arquitectos (AIA) por sus proyectos de vivienda.

Tocar, Inc., la firma de diseño interior, está compuesta por Susan Vendar y Christina Sullivan. Sus propuestas de diseño ofrecen un acercamiento fresco al concepto de elegancia, mezclando elementos clásicos y contemporáneos.

Roger Hirsch Architect (Roger Hirsch und Miryam Corti) entwirft vor allem Wohn-, Büro- und Geschäftshäuser. In den letzten zwölf Jahren konzentrierte sich das Büro besonders auf funktionelle und innovative Bauten. Dem Büro wurden zwei Preise vom American Institute of Architects (AIA) für seine Wohn- und Geschäftshäuser verliehen. Tocar, Inc., das Innenarchitekturbüro, wird von Susan Vendar und Christina Sullivan geführt. Ihre Gestaltungsvorschläge nähern sich auf erfrischende Art dem Konzept der Eleganz an, indem klassische und zeitgenössische Elemente gemischt werden.

☐ This interior, originally a six-room apartment in the center of Vienna, was converted into an open loft-style space for living and working. All the interior walls were demolished and the separation between the bathroom, the kitchen, and the bedroom was created with a single, red wall. The idea was to create two zones, one near the interior patio, where the single-function rooms are located – like the bathroom, the kitchen, and the bedroom – and another area facing the street containing a large multifunctional room where several activities can be carried out. The changeable character of this space depends on who is using it and what activities are taking place in it. An effort was made to ensure that the materials and the finishes of certain furnishings were related to the style of the original space. The kitchen table was made of concrete and covered with a natural resin. The bathroom floor is white mosaic tile, while linoleum was used in the rest of the private areas of the home. The original parquet was preserved, as were many of the building's original decorative details.

Small Loft in Vienna

› Lakonis Architekten

Vienna, Austria › 2002 › Photos © Margherita Spiluttini

☐ Lo que antiguamente era un apartamento de seis habitaciones en el centro de Viena fue convertido en un espacio abierto tipo loft para vivir y trabajar. Todas las paredes interiores fueron demolidas y la separación del baño, la cocina y el dormitorio se logró con una única pared de color rojo. La idea era lograr dos zonas, una hacia el patio interior, en donde se ubican las estancias más monofuncionales, como el baño, la cocina y la habitación;

☐ Eine ehemalige Sechszimmerwohnung im Zentrum von Wien wurde in ein offenes Loft zum Leben und Arbeiten umgebaut. Alle Innenwände wurden abgerissen und das Bad, die Küche und das Schlafzimmer durch eine einzige rote Wand abgetrennt. Es sollten zwei Zonen geschaffen werden, eine zum Innenhof, wo sich die Räume mit einer einzigen Funktion befinden, wie das Bad, die Küche und das Schlafzimmer, während die andere Zone, in der sich

mientras que la zona orientada a la calle alberga una gran estancia multifuncional que permite el desarrollo de varias actividades. El carácter versátil de este espacio depende de quienes lo habiten y de la actividad que se desempeñe en su interior. Se buscó que los materiales escogidos, tanto para los acabados como para ciertas piezas del mobiliario, tuvieran una relación con el estilo original del espacio. La mesa de la cocina se fabricó con hormigón y se recubrió con resina natural. El pavimento del baño es de mosaico blanco, mientras que en el resto de la esfera privada de la vivienda se utilizó linóleo. En la parte delantera de la casa se conservó el parqué original así como muchos detalles decorativos del edificio antiguo.

ein großer, multifunktioneller Raum für diverse Aktivitäten befindet, zur Straße liegt. Der wechselnde Charakter dieses Raums hängt von den Bewohnern und deren Aktivitäten in diesem Raum ab. Mit ausgewählten Materialien und bestimmten Möbeln wurde versucht, eine Beziehung zum einstigen Stil der Räume aufrecht zu erhalten. Der Küchentisch ist aus mit Naturharz beschichtetem Beton. Das Badezimmer ist mit weißem Mosaik gefliest, während die übrigen Privaträume Linoleumböden haben. Im vorderen Teil des Hauses wurden das Originalparkett und viele dekorative Elemente des Originalgebäudes beibehalten.

› Plan

› Planta

› Grundriss

1. What historical reference in particular inspires you when designing a residence?

¿Qué referente histórico en particular le sirve de fuente de inspiración a la hora de proyectar una vivienda?

Welche historische Referenz dient Ihnen als Inspiration beim Entwurf eines Hauses?

2. What is the main factor taken into consideration when designing a residence?

¿Cuál es el principal factor determinante a la hora de diseñar una vivienda?

Welche Rahmenbedingungen, bzw. Faktoren sind für Sie ausschlaggebend beim Konzipieren?

3. What room inside the home do you find most interesting to design?

¿Qué estancia de la vivienda encuentra usted más interesante para diseñar?

Welchen Raum des Hauses finden Sie am spannendsten zu entwerfen?

4. What is your criteria for choosing materials and finishings in a particular room?

¿Cuál es su criterio a la hora de seleccionar los materiales y los acabados en esta estancia?

Welche Kriterien wenden Sie bei der Entscheidung über Materialen und Oberflächen in diesem Raum an?

---

1. Buildings which invite us to use them in a new way: that can be large rooms like lofts in old factories as well as small rooms like the houses of Adolf Loos in Vienna.

2. To give people not only comfort, that is anyway important, but also to make them keen on discovering something new, like children in a barn.

3. It depends on how open the client is, so we are able to change the terms of each room.

4. The effect of materials depends on the way they are used. The unusual combination of well-known materials is often the way to spark people's interest.

---

1. Los edificios que nos invitan a habitarlos de un modo diferente: pueden ser desde amplios espacios tipo lofts en antiguas fábricas hasta pequeñas habitaciones como en las casas de Adolf Loos en Viena.

2. Ofrecer a la gente no sólo confort, que es importante, sino además despertarles la curiosidad en descubrir algo nuevo, como si fuesen niños en una granja.

3. Depende de cómo sea de abierto el cliente, nosotros seremos capaces de cambiar los términos de cada habitación.

4. El efecto de los materiales depende de la manera en que se utilicen. La combinación inusual de materiales bien conocidos es muchas veces la manera de despertar el interés de la gente.

---

1. Gebäude, die uns dazu einladen, sie anders zu benutzen, können große Räume im Stile der alter Fabriketagen oder kleine Räume wie in den Häusern von Adolf Loos in Wien sein.

2. Den Menschen soll nicht nur Komfort geboten werden, was sehr wichtig ist, sondern es soll auch eine Neugierde in ihnen geweckt werden, etwas Neues zu entdecken, so wie bei Kindern auf einem Bauernhof.

3. Je nachdem, wie offen der Kunde ist, sind wir dazu in der Lage, die Situation in jedem Raum zu ändern.

4. Die Wirkung der Materialien hängt davon ab, wie sie benutzt werden. Die ungewöhnliche Kombination von gut bekannten Materialien ist oft eine Form, um das Interesse der Menschen zu erwecken.

Mira Thal (Innsbruck, Austria, 1964) and Michael Buchleitner (Stuttgart, Germany, 1959) joined to found the architectural office of Lakonis Architekten in Vienna, in 1995. For them architecture is directly related to man's perception of the natural world, as well as being connected to the makeup of our cultural identity. In this sense, architecture fulfills both functional and economic requirements, by offering universal solutions for our environment. The firm offers a wide range of services, design, construction management, organization and budget management, in all phases of the project.

Mira Thal (Innsbruck, Austria, 1964) y Michael Buchleitner (Stuttgart, Alemania, 1959) se asociaron y fundaron la oficina de arquitectura Lakonis Architekten en Viena, en 1995. Para ellos la arquitectura está directamente relacionada con nuestra percepción del mundo, de igual modo que está relacionada con la conformación de nuestra identidad cultural. En este sentido la arquitectura da respuestas a exigencias funcionales y económicas para ofrecer soluciones globales a nuestro entorno. La oficina ofrece una gama de servicios, desde el diseño y dirección de obra hasta el control de presupuestos y organización del proyecto.

Mira Thal (Innsbruck, Österreich, 1964) und Michael Buchleitner (Stuttgart, Deutschland, 1959) gründeten im Jahr 1995 in Wien das Architekturbüro Lakonis Architekten. Für die beiden Architekten steht die Architektur in direkter Verbindung mit unserer Wahrnehmung der Welt und der Gestaltung unserer kulturellen Identität. Deshalb gibt die Architektur Antworten auf funktionelle und ökonomische Anforderungen, um globale Lösungen für unsere Umgebung zu bieten. Das Architekturbüro bietet umfassende Dienstleistungen, über Entwurf und Bauleitung bis hin zur Kostenüberwachung, Organisation und Überwachung aller Projektphasen.

This is the first phase, designed by the architects, for the transformation of the old Lords Telephone Exchange offices, in the center of London. The original structure of the building was ideal for creating urban living spaces on multiple levels, resulting in a project for 36 residential units, including 5 penthouses, which occupy the entire top floor of the building. The architects, in collaboration with Philippe Starck, were awarded the commission for the design and construction of this complex in a competition. This resulted in the creation of a series of unique, modern apartments, with fine details and finishes, within a plan that made the most of the structural and lighting conditions that already existed. Each living unit was based on the same concept: the creation of a unique and ample space for the living areas and independent areas for the kitchen, bedroom, and bathroom. A large variety of interiors were created in the eleven floors that make up the building, enriched by the changes in level, high ceilings, and exterior terraces.

Lords Telephone Exchange

› Paskin Kyriakides Sands

London, UK › 2002 › Photos © Paskin Kyriakides Sands

☐ Esta es la primera fase diseñada por los arquitectos para la transformación de las antiguas oficinas de la compañía Lords Telephone Exchange, en el corazón de Londres. La estructura original del edificio era ideal para la creación de un plan para espacios de vivienda urbana en múltiples niveles. El resultado fue un proyecto de 36 unidades residenciales, en el que se incluía cinco áticos que ocupan toda la parte superior del edificio. Los arquitectos

☐ Es handelt sich um die erste Phase der Umgestaltung des Unternehmens Lords Telephone Exchange im Herzen von London. Die Originalstruktur des Gebäudes eignet sich ausgezeichnet zur Schaffung von Stadtwohnungen auf verschiedenen Stockwerken. So wurden 36 Wohnungen geplant, zu denen 5 Dachwohnungen gehören, die den gesamten oberen Stock des Gebäudes einnehmen. Die Architekten gewannen die Ausschreibungen

ganaron el encargo del diseño y la construcción de este complejo gracias a un concurso, en el que contaron con la colaboración de Philippe Starck. Se obtuvo una secuencia de apartamentos en un estilo moderno y único, con finos detalles y acabados, dentro de un programa que saca el mayor partido de las condiciones estructurales y de iluminación con las que se disponía. En cada unidad de vivienda se partió de un mismo concepto: crear un espacio único y amplio para las zonas de estar y zonas independientes para la cocina, la habitación y el baño. En las 11 plantas que compone el edificio se crea una gran variedad de interiores, enriquecidos por los cambios de niveles, dobles alturas o terrazas exteriores.

für die Gestaltung und den Bau dieses Wohnkomplexes. Dabei wurden sie von Philippe Starck unterstützt. Durch die Planung entstanden eine Reihe von modernen und einzigartigen Wohnungen mit schönen Details und interessanter Gestaltung. Insgesamt wurde aus der vorhandenen Struktur und dem Licht der größtmögliche Nutzen gezogen. Jede Wohneinheit ging von dem gleichen Konzept aus. Man wollte einen einzigen und weiten Raum für das Wohnzimmer und unabhängige Bereiche für die Küche, das Schlafzimmer und das Bad schaffen. In den elf Stockwerken des Gebäudes entstanden sehr vielfältige Wohnungen, die durch verschiedene Ebenen, doppelte Höhe oder Terrassen bereichert werden.

› General plans
› Plantas generales
› Generalgrundrisse

0   3   6

› Plan
› Planta
› Grundriss

› Elevations
› Alzados
› Aufrisse

› Interior view
› Vista interior
› Innenaufsicht

Paskin Kyriakides Sands is a London firm founded in 1974 by Douglas Paskin, and it has grown to become a nationally known company thanks to the recognition received for its work. The firm specializes in urban planning, from modest new construction jobs to large urban renewal projects and master plans. Their main emphasis is the integration of the project into its surroundings, and strategic plans. They have vast experience in residential design, from luxury units to large apartment complexes.

Paskin Kyriakides Sands, firma fundada en 1974 en Londres por Douglas Paskin, ha crecido hasta formar una sociedad de fama nacional gracias a los reconocimientos por sus obras. La compañía está especializada en los planos urbanos, desde modestos proyectos de obra nueva hasta grandes reformas urbanas y planos maestros. Destaca la integración de la obra en el entorno y los planos estratégicos. Cuenta con una larga trayectoria en el diseño de residencias, desde unidades de lujo hasta grandes complejos de apartamentos.

Paskin Kyriakides Sands ist ein Unternehmen, das 1974 von Douglas Paskin in London gegründet wurde. Die Firma gewann durch ihre bekannten Projekte internationale Anerkennung. Das Unternehmen hat sich auf Stadtplanung spezialisiert, wobei sowohl Neubauten als auch große Renovierungsprojekte und Masterpläne durchgeführt werden. Die Unternehmensphilosophie basiert auf der Integration der Bauten in ihren Kontext und in die Stadtplanung. Man blickt auf eine langjährige Erfahrung im Bau von Wohnungen und Wohnhäusern zurück, angefangen bei luxuriösen Villen bis hin zu großen Wohnkomplexen.

□ The goal of this project was to convert an old shop on the ground floor of a building into a residence for the interior designer that collaborated with the architects on this project. Since the space was located between shared walls, the manipulation of natural light became the principal aspect of the design. It determined the form, the spatial distribution, and even the color of the project. The two existing façades were completely opened up with large windows that not only let the light into the interior, but also linked it with the exterior.

Sliding glass doors separating the centrally located bedrooms and bathroom allow light to enter and fully integrate them with the rest of the house. The pursuit of light is also reflected in the details, finish, and furniture. White is the dominant color in all the areas, and only a few specific pieces of natural wood stand out in this continuous uniform setting. A white façade and a white resin floor complete the picture, resulting in a home that is light and open, and in which the spaces are dynamic participants.

House in the Coast

› Joan Estrada / Special Events

Barcelona, Spain › 2003 › Photos © Nuria Fuentes

☐ El objetivo del proyecto era el de convertir un antiguo local situado en la planta baja de un edificio en una vivienda para el propio interiorista, que colaboró con las arquitectas en el desarrollo del proyecto. Puesto que el local se encontraba entre paredes divisorias, el aprovechamiento de la luz natural se convirtió en la principal condicionante de diseño, determinando la forma, distribución e incluso el color del proyecto. Las dos fachadas

☐ Es handelt sich um den Umbau eines ehemaligen Lokals in einem Erdgeschoss in eine Wohnung für den Innenarchitekten selbst, wobei die Architektinnen an der Planung mitarbeiteten. Da das Lokal von Zwischenwänden begrenzt wird, war das Tageslicht der wichtigste Faktor für die Planung, der die Form, Verteilung und sogar die Farben bestimmte. Die beiden bereits vorhandenen Fassaden wurden durch weite Fenster vollständig

existentes se abrieron completamente por medio de amplios ventanales que permiten no sólo el paso de la luz, sino el vínculo estrecho con el exterior. Las piezas centrales de la vivienda, los dormitorios y el lavabo, se dividen también a partir de puertas correderas acristaladas que permiten el paso de la luz y la integración total con el resto de la vivienda. La reiterada búsqueda de luminosidad se adivina también en los detalles, los acabados y las piezas de mobiliario. El blanco predomina en todas las zonas y sólo algunas piezas particulares de madera natural destacan de este marco continuo y uniforme que termina de definirse con la fachada blanca y el pavimento de resina blanca. El resultado es una vivienda clara y abierta en la que participan dinámicamente los espacios.

geöffnet, so dass einerseits viel Licht in die Räume dringt und andererseits eine Verbindung nach draußen hergestellt wird. Die wichtigsten Räume der Wohnung, die Schlafzimmer und das Bad werden ebenfalls durch verglaste Schiebetüren abgetrennt, durch die Licht fällt. So werden auch diese Räume in die übrigen Wohnungsbereiche integriert. Diese Suche nach Licht spiegelt sich auch in anderen Einrichtungselementen, Materialien und Möbelstücken wieder. Weiß ist überall die dominierende Farbe, und nur einige besondere Teile aus naturbelassenem Holz heben sich vor diesem einheitlichen und durchgehenden Rahmen ab. Sogar die Fassade und der Boden aus Kunstharz sind weiß. So entstand eine offene und klare Wohnung, in der die Räume dynamisch gestaltet werden können.

0 1 2

› Plan

› Planta

› Grundriss

1. What historical reference in particular inspires you when designing a residence?

¿Qué referente histórico en particular le sirve de fuente de inspiración a la hora de proyectar una vivienda?

Welche historische Referenz dient Ihnen als Inspiration beim Entwurf eines Hauses?

2. What is the main factor taken into consideration when designing a residence?

¿Cuál es el principal factor determinante a la hora de diseñar una vivienda?

Welche Rahmenbedingungen, bzw. Faktoren sind für Sie ausschlaggebend beim Konzipieren?

3. What room inside the home do you find most interesting to design?

¿Qué estancia de la vivienda encuentra usted más interesante para diseñar?

Welchen Raum des Hauses finden Sie am spannendsten zu entwerfen?

4. What is your criteria for choosing materials and finishings in a particular room?

¿Cuál es su criterio a la hora de seleccionar los materiales y los acabados en esta estancia?

Welche Kriterien wenden Sie bei der Entscheidung über Materialen und Oberflächen in diesem Raum an?

---

1. It is a cultural reference rather than a historic one. A combination of styles: Colonial, Asian, etc., that we use to create a special environment.

2. Light is a determining factor in the distribution of the rooms. Other important factors are maximizing the space and comfort in each one of them.

3. The kitchen. This is a multifunctional space that the residents enjoy at some time of the day. It has to be a clean, comfortable space, and above all very functional when it comes to fulfilling the customary tasks of this space. It is the inspiration for private or shared enjoyment. The kitchen is where part of life is cooked up.

4. The materials, as well as the space in general, should be functional and easy to clean: steel, glass, marble, wood. Porous materials should never be used.

---

1. Más que un referente histórico sería de carácter cultural. Una combinación de estilos: colonial, oriental, etcétera, con la que conseguimos un ambiente especial.

2. En la distribución de las estancias, la luz ha sido un factor determinante. También determinantes han sido el conseguir el máximo espacio y confort en cada una de ellas.

3. La cocina. Espacio multifuncional donde en algún momento del día los habitantes disfrutan de ella. Tiene que ser un espacio limpio, cómodo y sobre todo muy funcional a la hora de llevar a cabo las tareas que se desarrollan. La imaginación para el disfrute íntimo o compartido. En la cocina es donde se cuece parte de la vida.

4. Los materiales al igual que el espacio en general deben ser funcionales y de fácil limpieza: acero, cristal, mármol, madera, etcétera. En ningún caso materiales porosos.

---

1. Ich beziehe mich eher auf einen kulturellen Charakter als auf eine historische Referenz. Eine Kombination aus Stilen, kolonialer, orientalischer Stil, mit denen man eine ganz besondere Atmosphäre schafft.

2. Der wichtigste Faktor für die Verteilung der Räume ist das Licht. Ebenso wichtig ist es, so viel Platz und Bequemlichkeit wie möglich in jedem Raum zu schaffen.

3. Die Küche. Ein multifunktioneller Raum, von dem alle Bewohner irgendwann im Laufe des Tages profitieren. Es muss ein sauberer, bequemer und vor allem funktioneller Ort für die Aufgaben sein, die dort durchgeführt werden. Phantasie, um alleine oder zusammen zu genießen. In der Küche findet ein Teil des Lebens statt.

4. Die Materialien müssen, ebenso wie der Raum selbst, funktionell und leicht zu reinigen sein, Stahl, Glas, Marmor, Holz... Niemals poröse Materialien.

Special Events is an interior design firm founded by Joan Estrada in 1999, in Barcelona. His work mainly focuses, on the interior design of a wide range of projects, from commercial boutiques and shops, to homes, to high-design hotels. Single-family homes are the specialty of this firm, which carries out its work in several Spanish cities. The style is characterized by the purity of the spatial concept and attention to the smallest details.

Special Events es una firma de interiorismo fundada por Joan Estrada en 1999, en Barcelona. Su trabajo se centra principalmente en el diseño interior de una amplia variedad de proyectos, desde boutiques y tiendas comerciales hasta viviendas y hoteles de diseño. Las residencias unifamiliares son la especialidad de esta firma que desarrolla proyectos en varias ciudades españolas. Su estilo se caracteriza por la limpieza en la concepción de los espacios y el cuidado en los mínimos detalles.

Special Events ist ein von Joan Estrada 1999 in Barcelona gegründetes Unternehmen im Bereich Innenarchitektur. Estrada konzentriert sich hauptsächlich auf die Innenarchitektur von sehr verschiedenen Gebäudetypen wie Boutiquen und andere Arten von Geschäftsräumen, Wohnungen und Designhotels. Der Schwerpunkt des Unternehmens liegt in der Gestaltung von Einfamilienhäusern. In mehreren spanischen Städten wurden bereits Aufträge durchgeführt. Typisch für den Stil dieses Innenarchitekten ist die Klarheit der Raumkonzepte und die sorgfältige Ausarbeitung auch der kleinsten Einzelheiten.

LOFTS

LOFTS / LOFTS

□ This loft is located in a three-story structure built in the late nineteenth century, originally used for the manufacture of dental products. Beginning in the 1940's the building was used for artist's studios. The client's and the architect's original idea was based on creating a living and working environment, experimenting with different lighting, materials, and treatments of the space. The separation between the three different areas: an office, a meeting space, and living quarters was created using vertical expanses similar to trenches. These spaces were devised by removing part of the ironwork between the ground floor and the basement, and constructing an interior mezzanine. In doing so, the materials and characteristics of the industrial building were highlighted and a very dramatic interior space was created. The office and the meeting area, in contrast with the original rustic look of the brick and wood beams, were literally laid out as metallic islands surrounded by water.

Ling Office and Loft

› David Ling

New York, NY, USA › 2000 › Photos © Reto Guntli / zapaimages

☐ Este loft, ubicado en un edificio de tres plantas de finales del siglo XIX, fue construido originalmente como fábrica de productos dentales y a partir de 1940 se utilizó como estudio de artistas. La idea original del arquitecto y del cliente del proyecto partía de crear un entorno para vivir y trabajar experimentando con diferentes materiales, condiciones espaciales y de iluminación. La separación de las tres diferentes zonas del proyecto, una para ofici-

☐ Dieses Loft befindet sich in einem dreistöckigen Gebäude aus dem 19. Jh., das einst als Fabrik für Dentalprodukte errichtet wurde, und in dem sich seit den Vierzigerjahren Kunstateliers befinden. Die Idee des Architekten und des Kunden war es, eine Umgebung zum Leben und Arbeiten zu schaffen, in der mit verschiedenen Materialien, räumlichen Bedingungen und Beleuchtung experimentiert wird. Die Trennung der drei verschiede-

na, otra como zona de reunión y otra de vivienda, se logra a partir de espacios verticales, a modo de fosos. Estos espacios se lograron al eliminar parte del forjado entre la planta baja y el sótano y al crear un entresuelo dentro del volumen general. Mediante esta operación se sacó el mayor partido a las características y los materiales del edificio industrial al tiempo que se ha creado un espacio interior de gran dramatismo. En contraste con los materiales rústicos originales, como el ladrillo y las vigas de madera, la oficina y la zona de reuniones se diseñaron literalmente como islas metálicas rodeadas por agua.

nen Zonen des Gebäudes, Büro, Zusammenkünfte und Wohnen, wurde durch vertikale, grubenähnliche Räume geschaffen. Diese Räume entstanden durch das Entfernen von Teilen des Mauerwerks zwischen dem Erdgeschoss und dem Keller, so dass ein Zwischengeschoss geschaffen wurde. Damit hob man die Besonderheit und die Materialien dieses Industriegebäudes hervor und es entstand ein sehr dramatisch wirkender Innenraum. Als Gegensatz zu den rustikalen Originalmaterialien wie Ziegelstein und Holzbalken wurden das Büro und das Besprechungszimmer als eine Art von Wasser umgebene, metallische Insel gestaltet.

> Ground floor

> Planta baja

> Erdegeschoss

› First floor
› Planta primera
› Erster Stock

1. What historical reference in particular inspires you when designing a residence?
¿Qué referente histórico en particular le sirve de fuente de inspiración a la hora de proyectar una vivienda?
Welche historische Referenz dient Ihnen als Inspiration beim Entwurf eines Hauses?

2. What is the main factor taken into consideration when designing a residence?
¿Cuál es el principal factor determinante a la hora de diseñar una vivienda?
Welche Rahmenbedingungen, bzw. Faktoren sind für Sie ausschlaggebend beim Konzipieren?

3. What room inside the home do you find most interesting to design?
¿Qué estancia de la vivienda encuentra usted más interesante para diseñar?
Welchen Raum des Hauses finden Sie am spannendsten zu entwerfen?

4. What is your criteria for choosing materials and finishings in a particular room?
¿Cuál es su criterio a la hora de seleccionar los materiales y los acabados en esta estancia?
Welche Kriterien wenden Sie bei der Entscheidung über Materialen und Oberflächen in diesem Raum an?

1. Actually I am inspired by sculpture: Richard Serra, Eduardo Chillida, early Giacometti, early Noguchi, Anish Kapoor, Martin Puryear. Among architects I admire early Mies van der Rohe, Le Corbusier, Carlo Scarpa, Pierre Chareau, late Kahn.

2. For me the main factor is the physical idiosyncrasies of the space and the personal idiosyncrasies of the client.

3. I enjoy designing the entertaining space which for me is the kitchen/dining room since I design them together.

4. I like to juxtapose opposite materials and forms. Smooth against hard, rustic against refined.

1. Realmente encuentro inspiración en la escultura: Richard Serra, Eduardo Chillida, Anish Kapoor, Martin Puryear o los primeros trabajos de Giacometti y de Noguchi. Entre los arquitectos admiro las primeras obras de Mies van der Rohe, Le Corbusier, Carlo Scarpa, Pierre Chareau y las últimas obras de Kahn.

2. El principal factor es la idiosincrasia del espacio y la propia personalidad de cada cliente.

3. Disfruto diseñando un espacio divertido como es la cocina y comedor, ya que los diseño conjuntamente.

4. Me gusta la yuxtaposición de formas y materiales opuestos. Suave contra fuerte, rústico en oposición a refinado.

1. Ich werde wirklich von der Bildhauerei inspiriert. Richard Serra, Eduardo Chillida, Anish Kapoor, Martin Puryear oder die ersten Arbeiten von Giacometti und Noguchi. Unter den Architekten bin ich ein Bewunderer der ersten Werke von Mies van der Rohe, Le Corbusier, Carlo Scarpa, Pierre Chareau und der letzten Bauten von Kahn.

2. Der wichtigste Faktor ist die Idiosynkrasie des Raumes und die eigene, persönliche jedes Kundens.

3. Ich genieße es, unterhaltsame Räume wie die Küche und das Speisezimmer zu entwerfen, die ich beide zusammen entwerfe.

4. Ich liebe die Nebeneinanderstellung von gegensätzlichen Formen und Farben. Weich gegen stark, rustikal gegen elegant.

David Ling's multicultural background strongly influences his professional career. Brought up in the United States and educated in Europe, Ling still maintains his ties with China. After working as an associate in the offices of Richard Meier and I. M. Pei he established his own architectural office, David Ling Architects, in 1992. Ling defines the essence of his work as an artistic integration of space, form, light, and function enriched with materials. For Ling, all projects present a unique challenge, because of their diverse natures and variety of locations.

La formación multicultural de David Ling influyó en su carrera profesional. Creció en Estados Unidos y recibió su educación en Europa, pero nunca rompió con sus raíces chinas. Después de trabajar como colaborador asociado en las oficinas de Richard Meier e I. M. Pei, estableció su propia oficina de arquitectura, David Ling Architects, en 1992. La esencia de su obra la define él mismo como una integración artística entre espacio, forma, luz y función enriquecida con materialidad. Ling trata proyectos y lugares muy diversos de manera individual.

Die berufliche Laufbahn von David Ling ist erheblich durch seine multikulturelle Erziehung geprägt. Er wuchs in den Vereinigten Staaten auf, erhielt seine Ausbildung in Europa und ist durch seine Herkunft für immer mit China verbunden. Nachdem er als assoziierter Mitarbeiter im Büro von Richard Meier und I. M. Pei tätig war, gründete er 1992 sein eigenes Architekturbüro David Ling Architects. Er selbst definiert das Wesentliche seiner Arbeit als eine künstlerische Integration von Raum, Form, Licht und Funktion, die durch Gegenständlichkeit bereichert wird. Ling beschäftigt sich mit sehr verschiedenen Projekten und Standorten.

☐ This design project involved transforming an old industrial loft into a residence for a young family. The building, which originally housed a printing company, was recently converted into a residential building. The main goal was to preserve the magnificent views and sources of natural light present when the space was empty, while incorporating all the requirements of the new design. Concrete was poured to level the floor and to insulate it from the lower level acoustically. Walls for defining rooms were kept to a minimum, and a slightly lower false ceiling was added for certain lighting fixtures and to hide the utility installations. The main space of the loft has two central structures containing two bathrooms and a studio, which are covered with light wood and glass that lets light flow into the interiors. The configuration of these two elements defines the spaces and provides privacy where needed, while creating an interesting flow through the interior.

Light Loft

› Desai / Chia Architecture

New York, NY, USA › 2004 › Photos © Paul Warchol

◻ El proyecto consistía en la conversión de un antiguo loft industrial en una residencia para una joven familia. El edificio, originalmente utilizado como imprenta, fue recientemente convertido en un edificio residencial. El primer objetivo era el de conservar las magníficas panorámicas y fuentes de luz natural que el espacio ofrecía cuando estaba vacío, pero logrando incorporar todas las necesidades del nuevo programa. Se superpuso un

◻ Hier wurde eine ehemalige Fabriketage in eine Wohnung für eine junge Familie umgestaltet. Das Gebäude, in dem sich einst eine Druckerei befand, wurde komplett zu einem Wohnblock umgebaut. Hauptziel der Planung war es, den wundervollen Blick und die guten Lichtverhältnisse des leeren Gebäudes auszunutzen, aber dennoch alle für ein komfortables Wohnen notwendigen Räumlichkeiten zu schaffen. Es wurde ein durchgehen-

pavimento continuo de hormigón que sirvió para regular los niveles y crear un aislante acústico con la planta inferior. Las paredes que demarcan las estancias se intentaron reducir al mínimo y se creó un falso techo ligeramente descolgado muy útil para ciertos detalles de iluminación y para esconder las instalaciones eléctricas e hidráulicas. El espacio general del loft está estructurado por dos cuerpos centrales que contienen dos baños y un estudio y se encuentran envueltos por una ligera piel de madera y cristal que permite el paso de la luz a su interior. La posición de estos dos cuerpos permite la percepción total del espacio, pero al mismo tiempo sirve para delimitar y otorgar intimidad a ciertas zonas y crear un recorrido interesante en el interior.

der Betonfußboden über den alten Boden gelegt, um die Höhenunterschiede auszugleichen. Dieser diente gleichzeitig als Geräuschdämmung für die darunter liegenden Stockwerke. Es wurde versucht, so wenig Wände wie möglich zur Begrenzung der einzelnen Räume zu schaffen, und es wurde eine etwas tiefere, doppelte Decke eingezogen, die die Installationen für die Beleuchtung, Elektrizität und sanitären Anlagen verdeckt. Der allgemeine Raum das Lofts besteht aus zwei zentralen Körpern, in denen sich zwei Bäder und ein Atelier befinden, und die von einer leichten Haut aus Holz und Glas umgeben sind, durch die das Licht in das Innere dringt. Die Anordnung dieser beiden Körper ermöglicht eine Gesamtwahrnehmung des Raumes, aber gleichzeitig werden die Räumlichkeiten begrenzt und in bestimmten Zonen die Privatsphäre geschützt. So entstand eine interessante innere Struktur.

0 2 4

0 1 2

› **General plan**

› Planta general

› Generalgrundriss

› **Bathroom area plans**

› Plantas del área de baño

› Badezimmerhgrundrisse

› Interior elevations
› Alzados interiores
› Inneraufrisse

› Axonometry
› Axonometría
› Axonometrie

Desai / Chia Architecture was founded in 1995 by Catherine Chia and Arjun Desai in New York City. The architectural style of the firm is based on simplicity and an emphasis on the careful and articulated use of light and materials. Special attention is given to the roles of space and form in the design and function of each project. The firm is not given to excessive conceptualization; rather, it sees architecture as a field where tradition, innovation, and imagination should be present in proper measure.

Desai / Chia Architecture fue establecida en 1995 por Catherine Chia y Arjun Desai en la ciudad de Nueva York. La firma se centra en una arquitectura que busca la simplicidad con un énfasis en el uso cuidadoso y articulado de la luz y los materiales. El espacio y la forma están enlazados a una consideración detenida del programa y la función de cada proyecto. La firma no se esfuerza por un camino de excesiva conceptualidad, sino que entiende la arquitectura como un oficio en donde la tradición, la innovación y la imaginación deben estar presentes en su justa medida.

Desai / Chia Architecture wurde 1995 von Catherine Chia und Arjun Desai in New York gegründet. Das Unternehmen sucht mit seiner Architektur die Einfachheit, wobei besonderer Nachdruck auf den intelligenten Gebrauch des Lichtes und der Materialien gelegt wird. Bei allen Wohnfunktionen und auch der Gesamtfunktion jedes einzelnen Gebäudes werden Form und Raum berücksichtigt. Das Unternehmen versucht, nicht den Weg der übertriebenen Konzeptualität einzuschlagen, sondern seine Architektur als ein Handwerk aufzufassen, in dem die Tradition, die Innovation und die Phantasie in der richtigen Menge vorhanden sind.

☐ This project was a renovation of a loft in an old industrial building north of Tribeca, very near the Hudson River. The residence is on the third floor and has wonderful views of the river, which is dramatically different on weekdays than on the weekend. The long and narrow space had large windows on the west side and other smaller windows on the east side. The main objective of the renovation project was to reinforce the effect of the panorama and to take full advantage of the natural light in the interior. The flexibility and control of the natural light is achieved with 24 sliding glass panels. The combined living room, studio, and guest area was placed at the rear of the space, to enjoy the best lit area of the residence. Each one of these settings can be compartmentalized to form a separate unit, or joined into a single common space. Reflective materials, like steel and glass, direct the light to the least illuminated part of the residence, where the most private areas, the bedroom and the bathroom, are located.

DeBenedetto / Jiang Loft

› Smith and Thompson Architects

New York, NY, USA › 2001 › Photos © Doug Baz

☐ Este proyecto consiste en la reforma de un loft en un antiguo edificio industrial al norte de Tribeca, muy cerca del río Hudson. La vivienda está ubicada en una segunda planta y cuenta con maravillosas panorámicas del río, un paisaje que se muestra muy diferente en los días de diario que en el fin de semana. El largo y estrecho espacio tiene una sucesión de ventanas de gran formato en la parte oeste y otras más pequeñas, al este. El primer

☐ Die Planung besteht in der Renovierung eines Lofts in einem ehemaligen Industriegebäude im Norden von Tribeca ganz in der Nähe des Flusses Hudson River. Die Wohnung befindet sich in einem zweiten Stock und man genießt von ihr aus einen wundervollen Blick auf den Fluss, eine Landschaft, die sich an Wochentagen und am Wochenende ganz anders präsentiert. Es handelt sich um einen langen und engen Raum, der große Fenster nach

objetivo en el proyecto de reforma era el de reforzar el efecto de las panorámicas y aprovechar al máximo la luz natural en el interior. La flexibilidad y el control de la luminosidad se logran por medio de 24 paneles deslizantes de cristal. El área de la sala de estar, el estudio y la zona de huéspedes se ubica al fondo del espacio, aprovechando el sector más iluminado de la vivienda. Cada una de estas zonas puede ser compartimentada, formando una unidad por separado, o unidas en un solo espacio común. Los materiales reflectantes, como el acero y el mismo cristal, sirven para guiar la luz hacia la parte menos luminosa de la vivienda, en donde se encuentran las zonas más íntimas, como la habitación y el baño.

Westen und kleine nach Osten hatte. Das Hauptziel der Renovierung war es, den wundervollen Blick noch zu verbessern und das Tageslicht soweit wie möglich auszunutzen. Die Flexibilität und die Kontrolle des Lichtes erreichte man durch 24 verschiebbare Paneele aus Glas. Die Gruppe Wohnzimmer, Atelier und Gästezimmer liegt hinten im Raum, wo auch das meiste Tageslicht einfällt. Jede dieser Zonen kann unterteilt werden, so dass eine getrennte Einheit entsteht, oder mit den anderen zu einem einzigen Raum vereinigt werden. Reflektierende Materialien wie Stahl und Glas leiten das Licht in den weniger hellen Teil der Wohnung weiter, in dem sich die privateren Räume wie das Schlafzimmer und das Bad befinden.

0 1 2

❯ Plan

❯ Planta

❯ Grundriss

1. What historical reference in particular inspires you when designing a residence?
¿Qué referente histórico en particular le sirve de fuente de inspiración a la hora de proyectar una vivienda?
Welche historische Referenz dient Ihnen als Inspiration beim Entwurf eines Hauses?

2. What is the main factor taken into consideration when designing a residence?
¿Cuál es el principal factor determinante a la hora de diseñar una vivienda?
Welche Rahmenbedingungen, bzw. Faktoren sind für Sie ausschlaggebend beim Konzipieren?

3. What room inside the home do you find most interesting to design?
¿Qué estancia de la vivienda encuentra usted más interesante para diseñar?
Welchen Raum des Hauses finden Sie am spannendsten zu entwerfen?

4. What is your criteria for choosing materials and finishings in a particular room?
¿Cuál es su criterio a la hora de seleccionar los materiales y los acabados en esta estancia?
Welche Kriterien wenden Sie bei der Entscheidung über Materialen und Oberflächen in diesem Raum an?

---

1. We try to bring the sum of our travels and experience to each projects; also the particular local history and the vernacular are important to us. One of our recurring favorite historical references is Fatepur Sikra in Rajasthan, India. It seems relevant to all scales and types of projects.

2. Interpreting a client's program is the first creative step in a design. We then think of these ideas in relationship to the specific site.

3. Those spaces that share multiple functions as well as connector spaces between specific rooms.

4. Light and continuity.

---

1. Intentamos volcar la suma de nuestros viajes y experiencias en cada proyecto; asimismo, la historia particular y lo vernacular es importante para nosotros. Una de nuestras referencias históricas favoritas más recurrentes es Fatepur Sikra, en Rajastán, India. Parece relevante a cualquier escala y tipo de proyecto.

2. Interpretar los requerimientos del cliente es el primer paso creativo en el diseño. Es cuando entonces pensamos en estas ideas en relación con el lugar específico.

3. Aquellos espacios que comparten múltiples funciones así como los espacios conectores entre habitaciones determinadas.

4. La luz y la continuidad.

---

1. Wir versuchen, die Summe unserer Reisen und Erfahrungen in jede Planung einzubringen. Ebenso wichtig ist für uns die jeweilige Geschichte und volkstümliche Kultur. Eine unserer liebsten historischen Referenzen ist Fatepur Sikra, in Rajasthan in Indien. Sie scheint für jede Art und Größenordnung der Planung eine Rolle zu spielen.

2. Der erste kreative Schritt für die Gestaltung ist die Interpretation der Bedürfnisse des Kunden. Anschließend denken wir an diese Ideen im Zusammenhang mit dem spezifischen Standort.

3. Die Räume, die mehreren Funktionen dienen und die Räume, die verschiedene Zimmer miteinander verbinden.

4. Das Licht und die Kontinuität.

Smith and Thompson Architects is an architectural firm that was founded by G. Phillip Smith and Douglas Thompson in 1975 in New York. The office mainly designs residences, institutions, and commercial interiors. In 1989 they won a competition to do the construction of the East Hampton airport. They earned the Beaux Arch award for the design of the Kleeb residence, and the AIA Award for the design of the Jacques Marchais Tibetan Art Museum.

Smith and Thompson Architects es una firma de arquitectura fundada por G. Phillip Smith y Douglas Thompson en 1975 en Nueva York. La oficina desarrolla principalmente proyectos de vivienda, instituciones e interiores comerciales. En 1989 fue seleccionada gracias a un concurso para construir el aeropuerto de East Hampton y ha sido galardonada con premios como el Beaux Arch Award, por el diseño de la Residencia Kleeb, y el AIA Award, por el diseño de Museo de Arte Tibetano Jacques Marchais.

Smith and Thompson Architects wurde 1975 von G. Phillip Smith und Douglas Thompson in New York gegründet. Das Unternehmen plant hauptsächlich Wohnungen und Wohnhäuser, Gebäude für Institutionen und Geschäftsräume. 1989 gewann es die Ausschreibung für die Errichtung des Flughafens von East Hampton und ihm wurden mehrere Preise wie der Beaux Arch Award für die Gestaltung des Wohnhauses Kleeb und der AIA Award für die Gestaltung des Museum for Tibetan Art Jacques Marchais verliehen.

□ The challenge of this project consisted of transforming the structure of a rather small late nineteenth century industrial building, into a one-room residence that could also be used as a photo studio. Because of the small amount of usable space the approach consisted of keeping the intervention to a minimum, using only the pieces necessary for resolving the design, and preserving the original character of the space as much as possible. Recycled panels were used to cover the floor with a raised platform, mirroring the original surface and acting as an insulating space for the length of the room, and which contain the electricity and water installations. Two small areas were created, one for the bathroom and the other for laundry and storage. The placement of these two settings serves to divide the entire space into all its functional parts. The original details of the building were preserved whenever possible, and they stand out as an integral part of the interior design. Hand tools were used to help achieve the desired look in every case, for example, the refurbishing of the columns and beams and in the treatment of the exposed brick walls.

TB Guest Loft

› Tom McCallum, Shania Shegedyn

Melbourne, Australia › 2003 › Photos © Shania Shegedyn

El reto del proyecto consistía en transformar la estructura de una antigua nave industrial de reducidas proporciones, construida a finales del siglo XIX, en una vivienda de una habitación y que pudiera ser utilizada al mismo tiempo como estudio de fotografía. Como consecuencia de la mínima superficie disponible, la estrategia consistió en reducir al mínimo la intervención, incorporando únicamente las piezas necesarias para solucionar el programa,

Die Herausforderung bei dieser Planung bestand darin, die Struktur eines kleinen ehemaligen Fabrikgebäudes vom Ende des 19. Jh. in eine Wohnung mit einem Raum umzuformen, der gleichzeitig als Fotostudio benutzt werden konnte. Da kaum Platz da war, wurden so wenig Eingriffe wie möglich durchgeführt, und nur die notwendigen, funktionellen Elemente eingeführt, so dass der Originalcharakter der Räumlichkeiten weitgehend erhalten

y de este modo también conservar al máximo el carácter original del espacio. Se utilizaron tableros reciclados para cubrir el pavimento a modo de tarima elevada, recreando el suelo original del espacio y sirviendo de cámara aislante a todo lo ancho del espacio por donde pasan las instalaciones eléctricas e hidráulicas. Se crearon dos pequeños volúmenes: uno para el baño y otro para la lavandería y la zona de almacenamiento. La disposición de estas dos piezas sirve para dividir todo el espacio en todas sus partes funcionales. Se conservaron al máximo los detalles originales del edificio y se destacaron como parte integral del diseño interior. En todos los casos, como en la recuperación de las columnas y vigas, así como en el tratamiento de las paredes de ladrillo a la vista, se emplearon mecanismos totalmente manuales que ayudan a lograr el aspecto deseado.

blieb. Mit wiederverwerteten Holzplatten wurde ein Podium auf dem Fußboden gebaut. So wurde der Originalboden nachempfunden und gleichzeitig entstand eine Isolierschicht über dem ganzen Raum, durch die man die elektrischen und hydraulischen Installationen führen konnte. Es wurden zwei kleine Räume geschaffen, einer dient als Bad und der andere als Wasch- und Lagerraum. Diese beiden Räume sind so angeordnet, dass sie den gesamten Raum in seine funktionellen Bereiche unterteilen. Die Originalelemente des Gebäudes wurden so weit wie möglich erhalten und in die Innengestaltung miteinbezogen. Bei all diesen Arbeiten wie die Restaurierung der Säulen und Dachbalken und die Behandlung der Wände aus unverputztem Ziegelstein wurden handwerkliche Techniken benutzt, durch die man das gewünschte Aussehen erzielte.

Plan
Planta
Grundriss

0 1 2

› Interior elevations

› Alzados interiores

› Inneraufrisse

1. What historical reference in particular inspires you when designing a residence?
¿Qué referente histórico en particular le sirve de fuente de inspiración a la hora de proyectar una vivienda?
Welche historische Referenz dient Ihnen als Inspiration beim Entwurf eines Hauses?

2. What is the main factor taken into consideration when designing a residence?
¿Cuál es el principal factor determinante a la hora de diseñar una vivienda?
Welche Rahmenbedingungen, bzw. Faktoren sind für Sie ausschlaggebend beim Konzipieren?

3. What room inside the home do you find most interesting to design?
¿Qué estancia de la vivienda encuentra usted más interesante para diseñar?
Welchen Raum des Hauses finden Sie am spannendsten zu entwerfen?

4. What is your criteria for choosing materials and finishings in a particular room?
¿Cuál es su criterio a la hora de seleccionar los materiales y los acabados en esta estancia?
Welche Kriterien wenden Sie bei der Entscheidung über Materialen und Oberflächen in diesem Raum an?

1. There is no historic reference in particular however I employ a modernist design sensibility.

2. The main factor taken into consideration when designing a residence is respect to the original environment and pared back design where every single room is ergonomic, energy efficient and aesthetically beautiful to be in.

3. The bathroom.

4. A minimal and natural colour palette which mirrors finishes throughout the interior. In this case bluestone.

1. Ninguna referencia histórica en particular, aunque utilizo un enfoque del diseño modernista.

2. El factor más importante que tener en cuenta al diseñar una vivienda es el respeto por el entorno original y la creación de un diseño mínimo en el cual todas las habitaciones sean ergonómicas, energéticamente eficiente y estéticamente agradable.

3. El baño.

4. Una gama de colores mínima y natural que refleje los acabados en todo el interior.

1. Keine historische Referenz im Besonderen, obwohl ich mich auf das Konzept des modernistischen Designs beziehe.

2. Der wichtigste Faktor, der beim Entwurf einer Wohnung oder eines Hauses beachtet werden muss, ist der Respekt für die ursprüngliche Umgebung und die Schaffung eines minimalen Designs, in dem alle Räume ergonomisch, energetisch wirksam und ästhetisch angenehm sind.

3. Das Bad.

4. Eine minimale und natürliche Farbpalette, die Gestaltungselemente im ganzen Inneren unterstreicht.

The philosophy of the Tom McCallum design firm is to condense the practice into an essential search for beauty, ergonomics, and energy efficiency. To achieve a design that flows harmoniously, a systematic method is employed in every project, first analyzing the characteristics of the site, and later introducing the functional aspects. The design is always conditioned more by the ergonomic solutions for the use of the space than by decisions based on esthetics. Natural colors complement this Minimalist approach. This results in interiors that look spacious, that are easy to use, pleasing to touch, and visually calm.

La filosofía de la firma de diseño Tom McCallum es la de condensar la práctica en una búsqueda esencial de lo bello, ergonómico y energéticamente eficiente. Para lograr un diseño que fluye armónicamente los proyectos son abordados mediante un método en donde se analizan primero las características del lugar para luego introducir la funcionalidad. El diseño está condicionado más por soluciones ergonómicas de uso que por decisiones estéticas. Los colores naturales complementan esta ética minimalista. En consecuencia, se obtienen interiores prácticos, perceptiblemente amplios, atractivos al tacto y visualmente tranquilos.

Die Philosophie des Designbüros Tom McCallum verbindet die Aspekte Schönheit, Ergonomie und Ökonomie. Für die harmonische Gestaltung ihrer jeweiligen Projekte werden zunächst die Umstände jedes Ortes systematisch analysiert, dann werden die funktionellen Aspekte eingeführt. Deshalb unterliegt die Gestaltung immer den ergonomischen Aspekten der Benutzung des Ortes, aber sie basiert auch auf ästhetischen Gesichtspunkten. Natürliche Farben ergänzen das minimalistische Design. So entstehen leicht zu nutzende Räume, die weiträumig wirken, einladend sind und eine visuelle Ruhe ausstrahlen.

□ This loft, located in the middle of New York's popular Soho neighborhood, is home to a couple and their two small children. Despite the clients' desire to live in an industrial space in the center of the city, when faced with designing the space with the help of the architects they discovered several features that were inherited from previous conventional home layouts. Instead of creating an austere, white cube, they designed a space with more classical orders and sophisticated decoration. The result created a strong contrast between the existing architecture and the interior design. The layout of the residence is simple and easy to read: a central space, with dramatic windows illuminating the interior, contains the living and dining areas. A space partially divided by glass doors houses the kitchen while the two guest bedrooms are more independently located at the eastern side. The master bedroom, at one end of the residence, enjoys more privacy since it is separated from the central space by several very large shelves. Original architectural elements, like the columns, the system of beams, and the metal partitions on the façade, were emphasized in the space.

Loft in Soho

› Ziba Khalili, Alexandr Neratoff

New York, NY, USA › 2002 › Photos © Marina Berio, Jean Christian Bourcart

☐ En medio del popular sector del Soho de Nueva York se encuentra este loft que alberga una vivienda para una pareja y sus hijos pequeños. A pesar del deseo por parte de los clientes por vivir en un espacio industrial en el centro de la ciudad, al enfrentar el diseño del espacio con la ayuda de los arquitectos descubrieron múltiples necesidades que venían heredadas de sus previas residencias convencionales. En lugar de llegar a un cubo blanco y

☐ Mitten im berühmten Viertel Soho in New York liegt dieses Loft, in dem ein Paar mit seinen kleinen Kindern lebt. Auch wenn sie den Wunsch hegten, in einer Fabriketage mitten in der Stadt zu leben, entdeckten sie, während sie zusammen mit den Architekten den Raum planten, dass sie zahlreiche Bedürfnisse aus ihren vorherigen, konventionellen Wohnungen einzubringen hatten. So entstanden aus diesen Räumlichkeiten anstelle eines

austero, se llegó a un espacio de órdenes más clásicos y una decoración sofisticada. Se generó entonces un marcado contraste entre la arquitectura existente y el diseño interior. La organización de la vivienda es simple y de fácil lectura: un espacio central, con dramáticas ventanas que iluminan el interior, contiene las zonas de estar y comedor. Un espacio parcialmente dividido por puertas de cristal alberga la cocina, mientras que las dos habitaciones de invitados se ubican de forma independiente en la zona este. La habitación principal, situada a un lado de la residencia, logra una mayor intimidad al separarse del espacio central por medio de unas estanterías de gran formato. Se destacaron los elementos arquitectónicos originales del espacio como las columnas, el sistema de vigas y las particiones metálicas de la fachada.

weißen, nüchternen Würfels klassischere Räume mit einer edlen Dekoration. Dies führte zu einem starken Kontrast zwischen der existierenden Architektur und der Raumgestaltung. Ein anderer Raum, der teilweise durch Glastüren unterteilt ist, beherbergt die Küche, und die Gästezimmer liegen etwas unabhängiger im östlichen Bereich. Der wichtigste Raum auf einer Seite der Wohnung wirkt etwas privater, da er durch große Regale von dem zentralen Teil abgetrennt ist. Die originalen, architektonischen Elemente wie Säulen, Dachbalken und die Unterteilung der Fassade durch Metallelemente wurden erhalten.

0   2   4

› Plan

› Planta

› Grundriss

› Sections

› Secciones

› Schnitte

> Sections

> Secciones

> Schnitte

1. What historical reference in particular inspires you when designing a residence?

¿Qué referente histórico en particular le sirve de fuente de inspiración a la hora de proyectar una vivienda?

Welche historische Referenz dient Ihnen als Inspiration beim Entwurf eines Hauses?

2. What is the main factor taken into consideration when designing a residence?

¿Cuál es el principal factor determinante a la hora de diseñar una vivienda?

Welche Rahmenbedingungen, bzw. Faktoren sind für Sie ausschlaggebend beim Konzipieren?

3. What room inside the home do you find most interesting to design?

¿Qué estancia de la vivienda encuentra usted más interesante para diseñar?

Welchen Raum des Hauses finden Sie am spannendsten zu entwerfen?

4. What is your criteria for choosing materials and finishings in a particular room?

¿Cuál es su criterio a la hora de seleccionar los materiales y los acabados en esta estancia?

Welche Kriterien wenden Sie bei der Entscheidung über Materialen und Oberflächen in diesem Raum an?

---

1. [Z. Khalili]: My inspirations are the twentieth century, in particular the works of Le Corbusier, Louis Kahn and Ludwig Mies van der Rohe.
[A. Neratoff]: The Baroque in France during the 18th century, when a rarely innovation in small scale domestic architecture happened.

2. [Z. Khalili]: Different approaches to designing a house might be taken, nevertheless the relationship of a house to site remains the main generator of form.
[A. Neratoff]: The cultural framework, the clients' needs and cultural references, etc.

3. [Z. Khalili]: Any room, which has a mixed used function.
[A. Neratoff]: Any room that does not work out right away.

4. [Z. Khalili]: They are based on the design concept, function of the room, client preferences and creating a particular mood.
[A. Neratoff]: Their ability to define the shape of the three-dimensional forms they clad.

---

1. [Z. Khalili]: Mi fuente de inspiración es el siglo XX, en particular los trabajos de Le Corbusier, Louis Kahn y Ludwig Mies van der Rohe.
[A. Neratoff]: El barroco francés durante el siglo XVIII, donde hubo una peculiar innovación en la arquitectura doméstica a pequeña escala.

2. [Z. Khalili]: Se puede abordar de diferentes maneras; sin embargo, la relación entre la casa y el lugar sigue siendo el principal generador de la forma.
[A. Neratoff]: El marco cultural, las necesidades del cliente, las referencias culturales, etcétera.

3. [Z. Khalili]: Cualquier habitación que tenga un uso mixto.
[A. Neratoff]: Cualquier habitación que no se entienda como tal.

4. [Z. Khalili]: Están basados en el concepto de diseño, la función de la habitación, las preferencias del cliente y el generar un estado de ánimo particular.
[A. Neratoff]: La habilidad de los materiales para moldear la forma tridimensional que reviste.

---

1. [Z. Khalili]: Meine Inspirationsquelle ist das 20. Jahrhundert, insbesondere die Arbeiten von Le Corbusier, Louis Kahn und Ludwig Mies van der Rohe.
[A. Neratoff]: Der französische Barock im 18. Jahrhundert, wo es zu einer bedeutenden Innovation in der Architektur von kleineren Wohnhäusern kam.

2. [Z. Khalili]: Man kann an die Gestaltung eines Hauses auf verschiedene Weisen herangehen. Jedoch ist die Beziehung zwischen dem Haus und dem Ort der wichtigste Faktor für die Form.
[A. Neratoff]: Die kulturellen Rahmenbedingungen, die Ansprüche des Kunden, kulturelle Referenzen...

3. [Z. Khalili]: Jegliches Zimmer mit gemischter Nutzung.
[A. Neratoff]: Jeglicher Raum, der nicht als solcher verstanden wird.

4. [Z. Khalili]: Es basiert auf dem Konzept der Gestaltung, der Funktion des Raumes, den Vorlieben des Kundens und auf dem Hervorrufen eines besonderen Gemütszustandes.
[A. Neratoff]: Die Fähigkeit der Materialien, eine dreidimensionale Form zu schaffen, die sie verkleiden.

The Iranian architect Ziba Khalili grew up in Iran and pursued her professional education in France. After receiving a Master of Architecture degree she worked in Paris as an architect for several years. In 1986 she moved to New York where she studied sculpture, winning several prizes for her work. She founded her own architectural firm in 1990 and completed projects in New York and Paris.
Alexandr Neratoff is a native of New York and grew up in the community of Russian immigrants that was formed after the Russian revolution. He received his professional education in the United States.

La arquitecta iraní Ziba Khalili creció en Irán y recibió su educación profesional en Francia. Después de adquirir un máster en Arquitectura trabajó en París como arquitecta durante varios años. En 1986 se trasladó a Nueva York en donde complementó sus estudios en escultura y ganó varios premios por su trabajo. Fundó su propia firma de arquitectura en 1990 y ha desarrollado proyectos en Nueva York y París. Alexandr Neratoff es original de Nueva York y creció dentro de la comunidad de inmigrantes rusos instalados después de la revolución rusa. Su educación profesional la recibió en Estados Unidos.

Die aus dem Iran stammende und dort aufgewachsene Architektin Ziba Khalili absolvierte ihr Studium in Frankreich. Nach dem Studium arbeitete sie mehrere Jahre als Architektin in Paris. 1986 zog sie nach New York um, um sich als Bildhauerin weiterzubilden. Sie gewann mehrere Preise für ihre bildhauerischen Arbeiten. 1990 gründete sie ihr eigenes Architekturbüro und ist seitdem in New York und Paris tätig. Alexandr Neratoff stammt aus New York und wuchs in der Gemeinschaft der russischen Emigranten nach der russischen Revolution auf. Er besuchte die Schule in Frankreich und absolvierte sein Studium in den USA.

☐ This project was designed for a New York couple — one an art critic and the other a movie editor — living in the Hell's Kitchen neighborhood. The residence occupies an entire floor of an old industrial building, and has panoramic views of the city on three sides. The design highlights the industrial context, positioning new elements as if they were sculptures to complement the space and define the layout of the apartment. The result is a box, in which functions like the kitchen and the support areas are consolidated, defining the public and private areas of the loft. The oversize sliding doors that can be opened completely to integrate these areas with the rest of the space are an important element of the design. In general, the color white, the original polished concrete floors, and the exposed utility installations are the predominant elements that emphasize the character of the space. A collection of furniture and decorative elements in wood and soft textiles act as a contrast and create a comfortable environment.

Frank and Amy Loft
› Resolution: 4 architecture

New York, NY, USA › 2000 › Photos © Reto Guntli / zapaimages

☐ Este proyecto fue diseñado para una pareja, un crítico de arte y un editor de cine en el barrio de Hell's Kitchen de Nueva York. La vivienda se ubica en un antiguo edificio industrial, ocupa la totalidad de la planta de la estructura y cuenta con panorámicas urbanas extensas en tres de sus lados. El diseño realza el contexto industrial colocando elementos nuevos, de forma escultórica, que complementan el espacio existente y solucionan el programa de

☐ Dieser Wohnraum wurde für ein Paar, Kunstkritiker und Cutterin, im Viertel Hell's Kitchen in New York geschaffen. Die Wohnung liegt in einem ehemaligen Industriegebäude und nimmt ein gesamtes Stockwerk ein. Von ihr aus hat man einen wundervollen Blick auf die Stadtlandschaft auf drei Seiten. Die Gestaltung unterstreicht den industriellen Kontext und bringt neue, skulpturelle Elemente ein, die den bereits existierenden Raum

la vivienda. El resultado es una caja en donde se condensan los servicios, como la cocina y las zonas de apoyo, y define la esfera pública y privada del loft. Un elemento primordial de esta caja son las puertas correderas de gran formato que se pueden abrir completamente e integrar estas zonas al resto del espacio. En general, predomina el blanco, el hormigón pulido original del suelo, las ventanas existentes y las instalaciones a la vista; elementos que acentúan el carácter industrial del espacio. Como contrapunto, una colección de muebles y elementos decorativos de madera y suaves tejidos dan calidez y crean un entorno acogedor.

ergänzen und Lösungen für die Wohnfunktionen schaffen. Als Ergebnis entstand eine Kiste, in der sich die funktionellen Zonen wie die Küche und zusätzlichen Räume konzentrieren, und die die öffentlich und privat genutzten Bereiche des Loftes definiert. Ein wichtiges Element dieser Kiste sind die großen Schiebetüren, die völlig geöffnet werden können, um diese Bereiche in den übrigen Raum zu integrieren. Die im allgemeinen vorherrschende Farbe ist weiß, außerdem wurden die originalen, polierten Betonfußböden, die Fenster und die nicht unter Putz liegenden Installationen beibehalten, was den industriellen Charakter des Raumes unterstreicht. Als Kontrapunkt dient eine Sammlung von dekorativen Möbeln und Elementen aus Holz und weich wirkende Stoffe, die die Räume warm und einladend wirken lassen.

> Plan

› Planta

› Grundriss

> Axonometry

› Axonometría

› Axonometrie

› Model

› Modelo

› Modell

Resolution: 4 architecture is an architectural firm that was founded in 1990 in New York by Joseph Tanney and Robert Luntz. At the present time the company has a team of 10 people who have completed many projects of every size. Their work has earned them several awards including the AIA Award for the design of the offices of an Internet service provider, and a home for the architect Peter Eisenman, as well as the first place award in a contest to design a prefabricated house in Pittsboro.

Resolution: 4 architecture es una firma de arquitectura fundada en 1990 en Nueva York y compuesta por Joseph Tanney y Robert Luntz. Actualmente se compone de diez personas y ha completado una gran variedad de proyectos a diferentes escalas. Su obra ha sido merecedora de varios premios incluyendo los AIA Awards por el diseño de una oficina de servicios de internet, una residencia para el arquitecto Peter Eisenman y ganadores del concurso para el diseño de una casa prefabricada en Pittsboro.

Resolution: 4 architecture ist ein Architekturbüro, das 1990 von Joseph Tanney und Robert Luntz in New York gegründet wurde. Im Augenblick beschäftigt das Unternehmen 10 feste Mitarbeiter und hat bereits zahlreiche Projekte verschiedener Größenordnung durchgeführt. Dem Unternehmen wurden bereits mehrere Preise verliehen, darunter die AIA Awards für die Gestaltung eines Büros für Internetdienstleistungen, ein Preis für ein Wohnhaus für den Architekten Peter Eisenmann und den ersten Platz in einem Wettbewerb für ein Fertighaus in Pittsboro, NC.

☐ This residence is located in an old rope factory in New York. It had to fulfill two functions, those of being a home and also a studio. The interior space demanded a flexible approach to resolve a relatively complex structure. The solution was to create a system of translucent panels that act as dividing elements, shelves, and even as sources of light. These portable units cover the walls in some areas, leaning against the perimeter of the space, or they can be used to define enclosed spaces in the center part of the loft. The lightweight and translucent materials used in their construction allow this flexibility, and the natural light that mainly enters from the north can flow through them. The kitchen cabinets were designed using these same materials, while the kitchen countertop is concrete, cast in place and polished by hand, to match the overall esthetic sense of the residence. The bathroom was designed with an open floor plan, integrated into the rest of the space, with the different fixtures laid out separately. The system of panels allows the space to be adapted according to the requirements of home or work, or to make the interior look different when desired.

Giobbi / Valentino Residence

› Bone / Levine Architects

New York, NY, USA › 2002 › Photos © Jacek Kucy

Esta vivienda se ubica en una antigua fábrica de ropa de Nueva York y consistió en un programa dual, de vivienda y estudio, que permitiera alguna flexibilidad entre las zonas interiores solucionando una estructura relativamente compleja. Para solucionar esta premisa, se creó un sistema de paneles translúcidos que sirven como elementos divisorios, estanterías e incluso como fuentes de iluminación. Estas paredes móviles funcionan como

Diese Wohnung befindet sich in einer ehemaligen Kleiderfabrik in New York. Sie dient zwei verschiedenen Zwecken, als Wohnung und als Atelier, wobei zwischen diesen Zonen eine gewisse Flexibilität herrschen sollte, um die recht komplexe Struktur in Griff zu bekommen. Dazu wurde ein System mit durchscheinenden Paneelen entwickelt, die als Raumteilung, Regale und sogar als Lichtquellen dienen. Diese beweglichen Wände werden

revestimiento de algunas zonas, apoyándose en el perímetro del espacio, o pueden configurar espacios cerrados hacia las zonas centrales del loft. Los materiales con que fueron construidos, ligeros y translúcidos, permiten esta flexibilidad así como el paso de la luz natural que principalmente entra por el norte. Los muebles de la cocina fueron diseñados con estos mismos materiales, mientras que la encimera de la cocina es de hormigón fundido en obra y pulido a mano y se relaciona con la estética general de la vivienda. El baño fue diseñado como una habitación abierta, integrada en el resto del espacio, con diferentes elementos por separado. El sistema de paneles permite ajustar el espacio a las funciones de la vivienda o el trabajo, pero también convierte el interior en un ambiente siempre diferente.

als Verkleidung der Wandbereiche einiger Zonen benutzt, oder sie formen geschlossene Räume in den mittleren Teilen des Loft. Die Paneele sind aus leichtem und durchscheinendem Material. Sie sorgen für die gewünschte Beweglichkeit und lassen das Licht, das hauptsächlich aus der Nordrichtung kommt, hindurch. Die Küchenmöbel sind aus dem gleichen Material. Nur die Arbeitsflächen in der Küche sind aus gegossenem, handpoliertem Beton, was gut zur allgemeinen Ästhetik der Wohnung passt. Das Bad wurde als offener, in das gesamte Wohnambiente integrierter Raum angelegt, in dem die verschiedenen Elemente separat vorhanden sind. Durch das Paneelsystem können die Räume an die Funktionen Wohnen und Arbeiten angepasst werden und immer wieder aufs Neue neu gestaltet werden.

0 1 2

› Transversal sections

› Secciones transversales

› Querschnitt

Kevin Bone and Joseph Levine established their own architecture studio in 1982, with the premise that New York City's constructed environment presents special opportunities, as well as particular problems, for small architecture firms. The firm takes special interest in the materials and construction details that they introduce into their work. The projects strive to be simple, modern, and well constructed, with unexpected combinations of materials and sensitive detailing in their assembly.

Kevin Bone y Joseph Levine establecieron su propio estudio de arquitectura en 1982. Partieron de su creencia que el entorno construido de la ciudad de Nueva York presenta oportunidades especiales, así como problemas particulares para las pequeñas firmas de arquitectura. El trabajo de esta empresa toma interés en los materiales y los detalles constructivos para introducirlos en sus encargos. Obras que pretenden ser simples, modernas, bien construidas, con inesperadas combinaciones de materiales y empleando detalles sensibles en su elaboración.

Kevin Bone und Joseph Levine eröffneten ihr eigenes Architekturbüro 1982. Sie waren davon überzeugt, dass sich in der Umgebung von New York für kleine Architekturunternehmen interessante Möglichkeiten ergeben würden, und ganz besondere Probleme zu lösen wären. Die Firma brachte vor allem ihr Interesse an den Materialien und baulichen Details in ihre Arbeit ein. Es wurden einfache, moderne und hochwertige Gebäude errichtet, mit überraschenden Materialkombinationen und interessanten Einzelheiten.

› Directory

› Directorio
› Direktorium

Christoff:Finio architecture
250 West Broadway, 4th floor,
New York, NY 10013, USA
T: +1 212 219 1026
F: +1 212 219 9165
www.christofffinio.com

co-labarchitects
24/28A Hatton Wall,
London EC1N 8JH, UK
T +44 207 242 7255
F +44 207 242 7266
architecture@co-lab.net
www.co-lab.net

Fung + Blatt Architects
104 N. Avenue 56, Suite 3A, Los Angeles,
CA 90042, USA
T: +1 323 255 8368
F: +1 323 255 3646
contact@fungandblatt.com
www.fungandblatt.com

Gabellini Associates
665 Broadway, Suite 706, New York,
NY 10012, USA
T: +1 212 388 1700
F: +1 212 388 1808
www.gabelliniassociates.com

Alden Maddry Architect
928 Lorimer Street, Brooklyn, New York,
NY 11222, USA
T: +1 718 383 1947
am@aldenmaddry.com
www.aldenmaddry.com

Daniele Claudio Taddei
Feldeggstrasse 54, Zurich 8008,
Switzerland
T: +41 79 409 48 50
taddei@milnor.net

Gregory Phillips Architects
66 Great Cumberland Place,
London W1H 7FD, UK
T: +44 207 724 3040
www.gregoryphillips.com

Basil Walter Architects
611 Broadway, Suite 311, New York,
NY 10012, USA
T: +1 212 505 1955
F: +1 212 475 7320

David Ling
225 East 21st Street, New York,
NY 10010, USA
T: +1 212 982 7089
F: +1 212 475 1336
www.davidlingarchitect.com

Guillermo Arias + Luis Cuartas
Carrera 11 84-42, int. 5, Bogotá,
Colombia
T: +57 1 257 9501
garias@octubre.com.co
www.octubre.com.co

Bone / Levine Architects
561 Broadway, 8D, New York,
NY 10012, USA
T: +1 212 219 1038
F: +1 212 226 8056
www.bonelevine.net

Delugan_Meissl
Mittersteig 13/4, Vienna 1040, Austria
T: +43 1 585 36 90
F: +43 1 585 36 90-11
haasler@deluganmeissl.at
www.deluganmeissl.at

Holodeck.at
Friedrichstrasse 6/15,
Vienna 1010, Austria
T: +43 1 524 8133-0
F: +43 1 524 8133-4
vienna@holodeck.at
www.holodeck.at

Callas Shortridge Architects
3621 Hayden Avenue, Culver City,
CA 90232, USA
T: +1 310 280 0404
F: +1 310 280 0414
mail@callas-shortridge.com
www.callas-shortridge.com

Desai / Chia Architecture
54 West 21st Street, New York,
NY 10010, USA
T: +1 212 366 9630
F: +1 212 366 9278
www.desaichia.com

Insite Architecture Design
20 Rue de Billancourt,
Boulogne 92100, France
T: +33 01 41 10 22 70
F: +33 01 41 10 22 71
www.insitedsign.com

Camenzind Evolution
Samariterstrasse 5, Postfach,
Zurich 8030, Switzerland
T: +41 44 253 9500
F: +41 44 253 9510
info@CamenzindEvolution.com
www.CamenzindEvolution.com

Donald Billinkoff Architects
310 Riverside Drive 202-1, New York,
NY 10025, USA
T: +1 212 678 7755
F: +1 212 678 7743
yprokesch@billinkoff.com
www.billinkoff.com

Joan Estrada / Special Events
Vigatans 6, bajos, Barcelona 08003, Spain
T: +34 93 268 8614
F: +34 93 268 8615
joanestrada@joanestrada.com
www.joanestrada.com

John Wardle Architects
Level 10, 180 Rusell Street, Melbourne,
Victoria 3000, Australia
T: +61 3 9654 8700
F: +61 3 6954 8755
johnwardle@johnwardlearchitects.com
www. johnwardlearchitects.com

Jonathan Levi Architects
266 Beacon Street, Boston,
MA 02116, USA
T: +1 617 437 9458
www.leviarc.com

Lakonis Architekten
Rueppgasse 11, Vienna 1020, Austria
T: +43 1 216 0 215
buchleitner.thal@lakonis.at
www.lakonis.at

Leo Frei Architekten
Bergstrasse 50, Stäfa 8712, Switzerland
T: +41 1 926 7401
info@frei-arch.ch
www.frei-arch.ch

Marcio Kogan
Al Tiete, 505, São Paulo, Brasil
T: +55 011 3018 3522
F: +55 011 3063 3424
mk-mk@uol.com.br

Mark Mack Architects
2343 Eastern Court
Venice, CA 90291, USA
T: +1 310 822 0094
F: +1 310 822 0019
office@markmack.com
www.markmack.com

Page Goolrick Architect
20 W 22 Street, Suite 1505, New York,
NY 10010, USA
T: +1 212 219 3666
F: +1 212 414 5768
pg@goolrick.com
www.goolrick.com

Paskin Kyriakides Sands
7 Cliff Road Studios, London NW1 9AN, UK
T: +44 207 424 4800
F: +44 207 424 4801
info@pksarchitects.com
www.pksarchitects.com

Resolution: 4 architecture
150 W, 28th Street, Suite 1902, New York,
NY 10001, USA
T: +1 212 675 9266
info@re4a.com
www.re4a.com

Roger Hirsch, Myriam Corti
91 Crosby Street, New York,
NY 10012, USA
T: +1 212 219 2609
F: +1 212 219 2767
rhirschny@aol.com

Samuel Lerch
Eibenstr. 9, Zurich 8045, Switzerland
T: +41 1 382 4655
samnad@swissonline.ch

Sandra Aparicio + Forteza Carbonell Associats
Marià Aguiló 1-3, local 5,
08005 Barcelona, Spain
T: +34 93 307 6501
F: +34 93 307 6501
www.fortezacarbonell.com

Smith and Thompson Architects
501 West 26th Street, New York,
NY 10011, USA
T: +1 212 924 4358
F: +1 212 924 8917
smithth1@aol.com

tele-design
2-12-5 Mita, Minato-Ku, Tokyo, Japan
T: +81 3 3769 0833
F: +81 3 3769 9893
tele-web@tele-design.net
www.tele-design.net

Tom McCallum, Shania Shegedyn
shaniashegedyn@bigpond.com

Vicens + Ramos
Barquillo 29, 2° izqda., 28004 Madrid, Spain
T: +34 91 521 0004
F: +34 91 521 6550
vicensramos@arquired.es

Wood + Zapata
444 Broadway, 3rd floor, New York,
NY 10013, USA
T: +1 212-966-9292
F: +1 212-966-9242
www.wood-zapata.com

Yasushi Ikeda, Akiko Kokubun / IKDS
3-10-1 Aobadai, Meguroku,
Tokyo, Japan
T: +81 3 3461 3327
www.ik-ds.com

Ziba Khalili
307 East 89th Street Suite 4G, New York,
NY 10128, USA
T: +1 212 860 0112
F: +1 212 831 2859

Other titles by the publisher Otros títulos de la editorial Weitere Verlagspublikationen

La Fundición, 15. Polígono industrial Santa Ana. 28529 Rivas-Vaciamadrid, Madrid. Spain Tel.: 34 91 666 50 01 Fax: 34 91 301 26 83 asppan@asppan.com www.onlybook.com

Restaurantes al aire libre
Open-air Restaurants
ISBN (GB/E) 84-96048-20-9

Hoteles 100% Hotels
ISBN: (GB/E) 84-96241-80-7

+Hoteles. Designer & Design /
+Hoteles. Arquitectura y diseño
ISBN: (GB/E) 84-96137-14-7

Oficinas. Arquitectura y diseño /
Offices. Designer and Design
ISBN: (E/GB) 84-96137-57-0

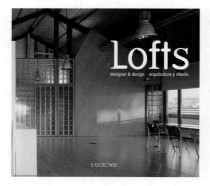

Lofts. Designer & design /
Lofts. Arquitectura y diseño
ISBN: (GB/E) 84-96137-16-3

MXM maximalist houses /
MXM casas maximalistas
ISBN: (GB) 84-96241-85-8
ISBN: (E) 84-96241-05-X

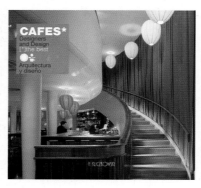

Cafes, the best
ISBN: (GB/E) 84-96241-70-X

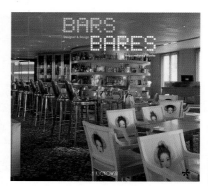

+ Bares. Arquitectura y diseño /
+ Bars. Designer & design
ISBN: (GB/E) 84-96241-06-8

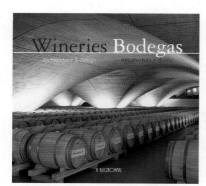

Bodegas. Arquitectura y diseño/
Wineries. Architecture & design
ISBN: (GB/E) 84-96241-78-5

XX Lofts. Designer and design/
XX Lofts. Arquitectura y diseño
ISBN: (GB/E) 84-96241-79-3

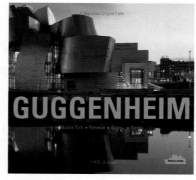

Guggenheim
ISBN: (GB) 84-89439-53-2
ISBN: (E) 84-89439-52-4
ISBN: (D) 84-89439-54-0

Gaudí. Complete works
ISBN: (GB) 84-96048-46-2
ISBN: (E) 84-96048-45-4

E: Text in Spanish / Texto en español / Text in Spanisch   GB: Text in English / Texto en inglés / Text in Englisch   D: Text in German / Texto en alemán / Text in Deutsch